Dea...

...y!

Andrea
xo

Dorcas Pelling

has written popular columns for *The Erotic Review* and *Grove Magazine*; she has also interviewed and written features and reviews for *Canary Magazine*, *Lotl Magazine Sydney* and *Time Out Sydney*, as well as being involved in the London literary salon Plectrum. Pelling lives in London with her partner and is about to start work with collaborator Sukie Smith on their first play.

how to be Irresistible

Dorcas Pelling

PAVILION

Contents

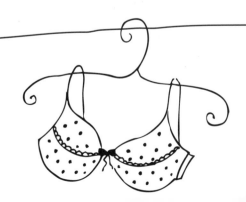

Introduction

"*Seduction is more sublime than sex; it commands the higher price.*"

JEAN BAUDRILLARD, FRENCH PHILOSOPHER

Welcome girls, and thank you for joining me as I take you on a sometimes informative, sometimes playful journey into the realms of flirtation, seduction and all things that help make a girl irresistible to boys. This book may not help you get Brad Pitt into bed, but it will certainly remind you that you have something no other girl has – your own unique allure – and this by its very nature will prove hard for certain attractive fellows to resist.

The more game, fun-loving and open you are, the greater your chances of successfully enjoying this book, and you'll also find attracting the object of your lust and affection all the easier. Win-win!

Whether making sure a suitor always remembers your lingerie size, or guaranteeing you charm your way to a pay-rise, this tongue-in-cheek guide should encourage you to embrace your sexiest attributes and adapt your thought patterns and behaviours to make conquests more entertaining and, importantly, victorious.

I hope you enjoy the ride.

CHAPTER ONE

Basic instincts

Before creating a truly staggering work an artist must first master the basics – the classic tools to improve their technique and lend an effortlessness to the finished article. Likewise a girl can only truly be a mistress of seduction if she studies and prepares for her encounters to ensure she artfully gets what she wants. A girl needs to think of her audience, her mood and how she wants events to pan out before turning her blank canvas into a hot piece – and although some of the most beguiling artworks took an age to create, there are few girls alive who can make a man lust more for them by delaying their grand unveiling for years. The basics are essential.

THE BEST GIRLS COME...
TO THOSE WHO WAIT

"I am invariably late. I tried to change but the things that keep me are too strong or pleasurable."
MARILYN MONROE

Temptations often arise to delay us for even very important dates, so make sure you have plenty of time to allow for any that might pop up and divert your attention. Likewise, punctuality has its merits, but does little to arouse anticipation in an awaitee. So offer your suitor just enough time to imagine your arrival before you finally, ahem, come. It's a delicate balance...

A bath can land a lady in very hot water when it comes to timekeeping. When a luxurious soak is coupled with pre-date excitement, one's mind can take over – instead of exfoliating, you might find yourself in the throes of the dirtiest fantasy you've ever had and forgetting all about the time.

Keep an eye on the clock, even if you feel pressurised by those pesky, ticking hands. It's important to be aware of how long you have for the stages of preparation. Time can be on your side later on if you find you have a delectable companion in tow. Then why not indulge in a game I like to call 'A Dangerous Method'. Lure him in with a pout worthy of Keira Knightly and have him recline on a leather couch. Ease out of your Freudian slip and swing your watch hypnotically from nipple to nipple. You'll unearth his darkest peccadilloes surprisingly quickly.

Wardrobe Prep

To cut down on prep time, set out your occasion-specific outfits that morning and limit the choices to suit your mood, your date and the impression you want to create. For example:

✳ An outwardly elegant and understated dress will lend you a demure air and with just a hint of black lace showing along the bustline you will certainly appeal to a chap who enjoys the finer things in life. On the outside you are conventional and refined, but this subtle hint of extravagant underwear will keep his imagination enthralled during your date.

✳ If you have a rendezvous with a hedge-funder go for the 'just out of the office' look – with a little artful adjusting it will help to raise your irresistible factor. Think Parisian chic cum Maggie Gyllenhaal in *Secretary*. Opt for a sharply tailored pencil skirt, seamed stockings and a crisp white shirt unbuttoned just so. Accessorise with a notebook filled with explicit yearnings and unforgivable typos. Take a red pen and see if he is up for showing you who is boss.

✳ If your suitor and venue are more edgy and laid-back, then you need to style out an outfit that is complementary to both. You can't go wrong with a pair of skinny black jeans, some sexy, studded ankle boots and a glamorously asymmetrical top. Accessorise with playfully gothic earrings and don't forget the smouldering eye make-up – a major turn-on for men!

For further date wardrobe ideas to help make you more enticing to your man, refer to Chapter Two.

Further Date-Delaying Preparation

Hours spent plastering on the slap holds you up massively and turns guys off. Keep things simple and find a look that makes the most of your features. Never experiment with a drastic new make-up look just before a date; the circus clown look only attracts a freakish type of man.

When it comes to intimate grooming, take a leaf out of the Chelsea Flower Show: exhibitors there know that for a desirable and winning (lady) garden the landscaping should never be rushed or last minute.

Playing music while you get ready is a great way to get you in the mood for the night's events, but the shorter your playlist the better, otherwise you'll find yourself so absorbed in indulgent choreography that you forget about the main event.

Transport Delays

'There is a good service on all lines' is a familiar announcement to all Tube users. However, as we all know, this doesn't guarantee a hassle-free journey; signals can fail, people can be taken ill and trains can break down. Your inner-carriage conduct can also waylay you. If you're feeling fruity and the only obvious hold-ups are ones you're wearing, it's still possible to miss your stop by engaging in distracting flirtations with an attractive commuter. Give yourself plenty of time to allow for any little diversions before getting back on track.

Even if it's a beautiful evening, avoid driving with your top down... Unless, that is, you actually have a convertible. Be mindful of other road users and stick to air-con to avoid causing any dangerous pile-ups.

Too punctual makes a girl look too keen. Though if you are running late, it is polite to alert him with a message, remembering that men respond best to direct words or explicit visuals:

'Not far off. Looking forward to seeing you. Am ravenous…x', and if you couple this with a visual of crimson mouth and an unsheathed lipstick laid softly at your parted lips, you will be instantly forgiven.

The Arrival

A preliminary inspection of your designated venue will allow you to locate the best place to make your entrance and a great first impression. It is advantageous to a girl to let a date see you can turn more heads than his alone. Offer him a solicitous smile and subtly loaded eye-contact to indicate your enjoyment at seeing him, to help put him at ease and to fire up the chemistry for the rest of the date.

Your approach should be slow and purposeful. Languidly slip your coat down your shoulders as you advance providing the effect of a mini striptease. Your movements should be deft and sensual, allowing him to glimpse more of your body. He will certainly stand to greet you, no matter how hard it may be.

IF HE IS LATE
Back-up plans are essential because weeping into your Gin Fizz is not the sort of activity befitting a seductress. If you are left *en sol*, why not savour a delicious Black Russian and finish with a Screaming Orgasm? Maudlin drunkenness has never made a girl sexy, but many happy hours can be found when indulging in more complex cock-tales.

THE ART OF PROVOCATION
— CAUSING A STIR

Getting a man's attention comes from stirring his interest and using certain approaches that arouse a strong reaction. Provocative girls are hard to ignore, they are neither obnoxious nor obvious, but rather types who are adept at creating intrigue and who dance dangerously close to the edge of what is considered to be decent behaviour.

Here are the basic aims of provocation:

✳ *Be Visual:* 'Accidental' wardrobe malfunctions should be spectacular and deliberate if you wish to get a suitor hot under the collar. Wearing a wrap dress that unfurls for a split second as you slink by should reveal just enough to put his gallantry to the test.

✳ *Be Different:* We are each unique and need to enhance what makes us stand out from the crowd. If you're a statuesque beauty, never be physically apologetic, but instead embrace your Amazonian allure and become the type of girl who would only ever stoop to conquer.

✳ *Be Daring:* Go outside of your comfort zone and embrace new experiences. Boys love a girl who is up for anything.

✳ *Inspire Curiosity:* Divulge an unusual ability or tell him about a dangerous hobby you love. If there is more to you than meets the eye, letting a chap know will pique his interest... Curiosity may have killed the cat, but it's always been a friend to the pussy.

✳ *Pose a Challenge:* If your date is something of a Don Juan and women come easily to him, you should prove the exception. Let him know you can be won but you won't make it easy for him – instead set the pace for the pursuit. Men enjoy most the pleasures they have to work for.

✳ *Be Fun:* Men love a little, ahem, light relief and when it comes to seduction, even if your aims are serious, you need to keep things a little playful.

✳ *Embrace Scandal:* When faced with adversity, channel Christine Keeler (the notorious 60s sex siren); disrobe, dismiss all sexual politics and straddle your desired suitor.

✳ *Thought-Provoking:* Start a scurrilous rumour about yourself and see how long it takes before an admirer begs to be shown the tricks you learnt from the courtesans of Shanghai.

✳ *Dare to Disagree:* Having strong convictions is sexy, it shows that you have your own mind and showcases passion... that or you have an impressive criminal nature.

✳ *Reactionary:* Make him jealous and have a strip-poker night with the girls, remembering to lock the door. His eyes will be glued to the keyhole and he'll long for a game of five-card stud.

(If all else fails, shock him into life with electrodes placed on sensitive areas of his body!)

SINDERELLA: LEAVE THEM WANTING MORE

A well-timed exit maximises the potency of your personal mystique. For sheer decadence pay homage to Cinders, that dirty little scrubber, and leave an exotic calling card. Prince Charming will soon pursue you for a feverish encounter that sees him morph into a delightfully uncouth Beast.

How to Enrapture Your Audience

SOCIAL INTERCOURSE

It is important to engage a man's mind as their bodies are only too willing to be led astray. Seducing with any longevity in mind requires intellectual stimulation, so you need to be surprising, challenging and visual. In order to keep a man spellbound by a story you are telling, it must include surprising and descriptive twists which make him want to get to know you better. If you're mad about bee-keeping, droning on about the plight of the worker bee will result in most men glazing over. In this instance, the example below would get results:

1. Start with a vivid description of the first sticky comb you retrieved from a hive and the viscous nectar you found there. How incredible the taste of it was on your fingers.

2. Increase the intimacy of your exchange by leaning into him. Tease him by saying that, if harnessed in a large test tube, all those powerful, buzzing little creatures would create an awesome natural vibrator. He certainly won't have been expecting that and now will be thinking of sex.

THE EXIT

It is best to depart when you know you have your audience suitably warmed up and longing for something hotter. There is erotic power to be gained for both parties in suggesting an encore at a later date, and men find it impossible not to go after someone they want but have not yet won.

When bidding farewell to a group of people, leave your favoured suitor till last, seemingly as an afterthought, but be sure to do something that will keep you in his mind. Cinderella may have chosen a vertiginous Louboutin, but even if he is a shoe fetishist, frankly no man is worth such a dent in a lady's wardrobe. Instead try one of the below or create your own unique exit act to make sure you remain in his thoughts:

✳ Bite the side of his neck gently and whisper 'the way I want to kiss you would not be suitable in polite company'.

✳ Kiss him on the side of his mouth. This oft-neglected zone crackles with electricity when brushed 'accidentally' by tantalising lips.

✳ Lipstick on a man's collar is so passé; instead lead him to a private place and leave an imprint of yourself somewhere more intimate.

✳ Get your message over loud and clear by slipping your knickers, adorned with your mobile number, into his coat pocket. The resulting chase will be 'off the hook'.

Porky Pies: More Appetising than the Truth?

There is a tendency in all individuals to do a little bit of up-selling when trying to land a lover, but it's best to avoid whoppers, at least of the lying variety. The bigger the lie, the greater the effort to untangle yourself. Eventually someone will call you on it and, if they have a sense of humour failure, your date will be memorable for all the wrong reasons.

BLAGGING IT: LIES ABOUT YOURSELF

✳ 'I used to be an exotic dancer' is fine, as 'exotic' lends itself to certain artistic licence. Even if you mean Irish dancing, you can still make it sexy. Remember those constrained upright movements and controlled powerful kicks will be more appealing if you pour lashings of Jameson's down your body as you perform.

✳ 'I'm only twenty-five': lying about age is not an uncommon tendency for us girls. However, not only do you have to prep potential blabbers on the lie, but you may need to hide all your personal documentation and real birthdays soon become a nightmare. There is something far sexier about a woman who relishes her age and all the experiences each year brings.

✳ 'I love football too' is dangerous if what you really mean is 'I love footballers' thighs and stamina'. This lie allows a man to become very specific in his acts of romance. Do you really want him to gift you with a highly flammable football strip rather than saucy lingerie? Your ideas of what the 'beautiful game' means may prove wildly different.

✳ 'Oh, you know, the average amount': if asked by an inquisitive suitor how many partners you have had, do not intimidate him, nor should you pretend to be the Virgin Mary. Men's egos are fragile commodities, they want to be the best and preferably the first. Handle their delusions carefully but firmly.

✳ If you like your sexual encounters risqué and short-lived, this one will work a treat: 'I am saving my vagina for marriage'.

✳ 'I love it': if he is uncut and it's not your thing, at least give him a chance, his aesthetically unappealing pride and joy may yet give him pride, and you joy.

✳ 'Yes, it's the biggest I have ever had': boys need to believe they have the largest toys, whether plasma screens or cocks. And this is an acceptable lie if you compare said toy with something smaller in your head.

✳ 'No, I have never done this before': he may be all excited about introducing you to a new sensory experience, and even if you have a gold star in the chosen 'activity', indulge him and approach it with the enthusiasm of a first-timer.

✳ 'Please stop worrying. I like that you find me so exciting': sometimes an early arrival is the fate of an eager fellow. Though it may be a let-down for you, you can be sure he will feel more withered.

TROUBLE WITH A CAPITAL TEASE:
STICKY SITUATIONS

In life, a little seductive mischief can help turn a potentially unpleasant situation into something much more gratifying.

Tricky patient: An X-rated game of doctors and nurses may not cure your under-the-weather lover of anything, but by playing sexy nurse you could perk him up no end. You won't be surprised just how high up on the list of male fantasies this rates, and you can have fun and be in charge in a subtle way. If anything, it may highlight how sick you can both actually be! If you are both really getting into it, take things up a notch with the snap of a rubber glove and a more thorough examination of your patient's body. Whisper in his ear: 'I think an injection is in order' as you eye his engorged member and add 'I think one of us is going to feel a BIG prick' before offering a feigned look of trepidation. There's a lot to be said for a bedside manner.

Walk of shame: Just testing. Shame is for amateurs!

Running into an ex: If at all possible, plan this one girls. If you hear that a certain someone from your past will be at the same event as you, make sure you are dressed to kill and surround yourself with a bevy of hot men. You want your old flame to see how happy, successful and in demand you are. If it was a really bad break-up, perhaps next time you run into him you could use a car... (make sure you have a good lawyer).

Going down? If you find yourself in an elevator that is stuck between floors for an indefinite period, don't despair. It is in times like these that a girl can have a very interesting encounter indeed. Several hours of privacy and intensity in a small space is a perfect opportunity for naughtiness. Of course you can't have this experience with just anyone (even if there has been a power cut there is only so much that darkness can hide), but remember: what happens in the lift, stays in the lift.

If you develop a taste for this sort of thing, who's saying you couldn't become an expert lift-tamperer and choose exactly who to get 'stuck in' with?

'JE NE REGRETTE RIEN': APOLOGISING

Expressing your sincere regret for a transgression comes down to how wronged the other party feels. However bad you've been, you should always be able to increase the power of your apology with something equally naughty.

Buying flowers for a man is a bold statement and can be highly effective in winning back his affections, especially if the bouquet is made of edible blooms placed strategically on your body. A man secure in his sexuality would be suitably disarmed by this thoughtful floral arrangement.

If you've the kind of man who is impressed with extravagance and you really, really need to show him how sorry you are, how about a well-executed performance to do just that? Try abseiling down his apartment building and into his bedroom like a Bond girl, before flashing your licence to thrill. No man could stay angry when confronted with Pussy Galore.

If all else fails, get down on your hands and knees and kiss his feet. Work your way up. Whatever blow your transgression served will prove no match for the blow you can offer as an apology. If even this doesn't work and there is no other recourse, you could always let him do that thing you don't like... unless it involves golf.

If you apologise using every inch of your well-bred body and still forgiveness is denied, he clearly doesn't deserve one.

CHAPTER TWO

The Devil wears
Prada, the seductress
wears a grin

"I have a dress-up chest at home.
I love fantasy."

KATE MOSS

ARMOURY APPLICATION: PREPARING FOR THE SEDUCTION BATTLEFIELD

All's fair in love and war, but in seduction a girl is often more winning if she has subtly prepared her look to hit below a man's belt. A soldier doesn't just go into battle and hope for the best; no, he prepares, he has a tactical plan of how he can best penetrate his target's defences. He dresses for action. He arms himself with knowledge and suitable weaponry to guarantee victory. Finally he psyches himself up, because he knows that to be triumphant you can't go into combat holding thoughts of failure. Girls who follow these examples when getting ready for a seductive offensive will never be short of action.

General Preparation

It never hurts to do some homework on your date, and thanks to social networking you can research your target, his interests, his style, friends and ex-lovers before you meet.

You need to be in the right frame of mind when getting ready, because if you are indecisive or in a slightly defeatist mood, it will lead to poor clothing choices and you'll give off the wrong attitude to your date. Instead meditate on sexy and positive affirmations to boost your confidence.

A sure-fire way to improve your mood is with a little pre-date exercising. Ten minutes of rigorous exertion will recharge your endorphins and stimulate body confidence and sexiness. Think of this session as a pre-coital warm-up!

When dressing, be tactical. Your undergarments must be first and foremost chosen to help you feel delectable and indestructible, and though their effect on a lover is also important, that is certainly their secondary concern.

Don't forget that your legs should arouse explosive admiration in a suitor so pay special attention to waxing those pins, moisturising, and never scrimp on stockings.

Only choose one asset to showcase on a date. Assaulting a man's senses with tits, arse and legs all at once could hospitalise him if he has a weak heart.

If you are wearing something that would be ruined by VPL, or if the mood takes you, then go sans knickers! If you want to up the ante, you could always alert him to the fact later on in the night.

Ask yourself what sort of dresser he is. Is he a hipster, dandy or rugger-bugger? Try to complement a man's look without being slavish. He will feel instantly more relaxed around you and it increases the chances that he will see you as a compatible match. If you know that he always wears skater jeans and a baggy T-shirt, turning up in an evening gown will make you both uncomfortable and you'll look ridiculous together.

A seductress, unlike a soldier, should never try to camouflage herself otherwise she will be lost in the crowd. A girl is most magnetic to men when she's dressed and poised, to guarantee she feels comfortable, powerful and hot.

Scent is important. Smelling incredible helps to draw people to you just as smelling awful repels people. Your signature fragrance should work with your natural scent rather than masking it. The undertones of your pheromones when combined with high notes of floral or musk help make you irresistible to a man.

Remember, dating can be intense girls and the better rested you are, the more stamina you'll have for any all-night encounters.

What Do You Want Your Outfit to Say About You?

Remember that what you wear gives others information about the type of girl you are. It's said you shouldn't judge a book by its cover but let's face it, most people do. Men will still approach a woman if she has stains on her clothes, or is wearing a cheap-looking skirt, but that isn't necessarily because he is less shallow; he might just see a girl as easy game because he has read her as someone who doesn't value how she looks.

You don't need to be in expensive designer clothing to attract men but, and this may sound obvious, to ensure a great first impression, whatever your style, your outfit should be clean, suit your shape and fit you properly. This is basic but vital when you want to attract someone.

Never be overly complicated when dressing – frills, pleats and intricate detailing may be your way of showing what a whimsical and multi-faceted creature you are, but trust me, no man sees that!

If you want a man to take you seriously, never wear a hat with animal ears, or sport pigtails or anything that would be found in the wardrobe of a Japanese schoolgirl.

Polished, unique and approachable is the optimal message a girl can send to a man with her clothing, especially if that outfit hints at what lies beneath. Whatever you wear should make you feel powerful enough to inspire a man to submit to your will. The more confident and sexy you feel in your attire, the greater your pulling power will be.

Some may say it's not what you wear, rather how you remove it. Either way, the devil is in the detail and it would be a sin not to do yourself justice in both areas.

Here are some saucy wardrobe ideas to inspire you. But remember the most powerful look a girl can pull off is one that is true to her own unique style:

✴ If you are a retro girl, a polka-dot, bias-cut dress with seamed stockings and peep-toe heels is the perfect look to grab the attention of a man who favours old-fashioned courtship.

✴ Wearing leather helps to bring out the animalistic magnetism in a girl. It's tactile, sexy and hints that the wearer should not be messed with. One statement leather garment gives a girl a dirty rock-chick edge, but anything more screams Posh and Becks circa 1996.

✴ If you fancy yourself as the first lady of seduction, think Carla Bruni-Sarkozy and go for a sharp, chic tailored suit and equip yourself with a ruthless demeanour. Beware – this look may prove an aphrodisiac to small but powerful men.

✴ To be fatally attractive, a tactile V-neck cashmere jumper cut a tad low is perfect for showing off magnificent breasts. This, quite frankly, will make a man want to rut like a rabbit and death by décolletage is far more pleasing to a bloke than being boiled in a pot.

✴ If you have an enticing ass(et) then remember the old (paraphrased) adage that 'one lady's junk is, well, every man's treasure'. A rear-enhancing skirt will ensure you generously share the wealth, and men who see you will be overcome by greed.

✴ For showcasing the natural look, what could be more irresistibly 'ready-to-wear' than a girl clad in absolutely nothing? Obviously this look is not suitable for all occasions, alas...

No-Man's-Land – The Secrets of Handbags

"A woman's mind is as complex as her handbag, there are always surprises at the bottom."
BILLY CONNOLLY

For girls, handbags are fetishistic, sacred vestiges protecting everything they hold dear, and delving into one can expose darker secrets than those found in Pandora's box.

Mary Poppins was the original pioneer of the deceptively seductive bag. Hers, to the naked eye, was unremarkable, but proved a labyrinth of exquisite toys and sorcery. She wasn't a slave to fashion and knew the secret of getting things to 'go down in the most delightful way'. Such qualities should be revered by girls worldwide.

Bear in mind that heaving about an enormous bag that's as sought after as a multiple orgasm doesn't go down well on a date. It won't so much suggest 'overnight bag' to a suitor as 'let's move in together'. The only Birkin men find sexy answers to the name of Jane and would certainly assault you if you attempted to put your keys in her. Actual baggage and emotional baggage have the same effect on men; the more of it there is on display, the more readily he will want to back off.

Rocking the 'sans bag' look is perfect for the adventurous girl, especially if you have a sexually secure boy in tow to keep your belongings on his person. He'll enjoy that added bulge in his trouser pocket even if you are disheartened when you remember the reason it's so enhanced.

If you can't do without a bag make sure you regularly clear it out, as excess crap cluttering its interior isn't sexy. Make sure the contents are things that, if required, aid seduction.

✳ *Phone:* Essential to remaining upwardly mobile, with suitors on speed-dial and messages worthy of hacking.

✳ *Business cards:* Made from expensive, sensual materials, adorned with simple lettering and saucy artwork, these make a man want to attend to some nocturnal business.

✳ *Purse:* Keep coins for tipping, notes for stripping and plastic for breaking and entering.

✳ *Passport, map and dart:* Unusual perhaps, but a sense of adventure is advantageous in ALL areas.

✳ *Keys:* You never know what type of party you'll end up at.

✳ *Compact:* Practical for reverse-view flirting.

✳ *Disco wipes and toothbrush:* If you want to get fresh, you should always make sure you are fresh.

✳ *Perfume:* Olfactory arousal helps stimulate sexual appetites.   27

✳ *Polaroid/digital camera:* 'Blackmail' is such an ugly word, why not use 'visual persuasion'?

✳ *Knickers:* In the throes of passion caution goes out of the window and sometimes lingerie follows.

✳ *Sunglasses:* A lady should always carry some protection.

✳ *Novel approach:* Reading gives a woman pulling power by allowing a man to approach her on the pretext that he is interested in her book. Open *Lady Chatterley's Lover* and soon a man will appear wanting to know what it's like.

✳ *Foreign phrase book:* Very useful for attracting the opposite sex; boys love a girl with an accent.

✳ *Toys:* For advanced encounters only...

KILLER HEELS — LIFE-ENHANCING FOOTWEAR

"I was born in high heels and I have worn them ever since."
HELENA CHRISTENSEN

The slow, measured click of a finely crafted stiletto as it connects with concrete on a sleepy street is choicely satisfying to a girl and sufficient to give a man a hard-on. Heels are the ultimate in sexy footwear not least because they are sophisticated, difficult to master and as with breasts, stockings and vaginas, men don't have them and are helpless to resisting their power.

A perfect heel's job is to tilt a lady to a degree that makes her derrière jut outwards just so, her tits push forward and the muscles in her legs tighten. The resulting effect is that of a woman's body looking taut, alive and primed for action. This sight is irresistible to men.

Heels demand you sway your hips in a forward motion as hypnotically as a slinking snake, allowing assured, balanced and seductive movement. The more practised you are in them, the quicker you will be able to give Christina Hendricks in *Mad Men* a run for her money.

Heels offer a girl the most attractive form of S&M as the wearer is singularly in charge of her own bondage. Even though heels give the impression that the wearer is vulnerable, in truth they transform her into a force to be reckoned with.

Head for Heights

If you find a pair of heels that you yearn for but seem impossible to manoeuvre in, do not be put off, some footwear lends itself very attractively to more horizontal activities. These vertiginous numbers are perfect for digging into a paramour's straining, thrusting glutes when a girl is reclined. If you don't take things lying down, why not slip the pretty but tricky heels on and bend invitingly over the bed, as your date proves what a rigid connoisseur he can be?

If a boy is keen you follow after him, these shoes prove marvellous aids to increased sexual tension because they ensure a girl cannot be so easily moved. If he seems perplexed as to why you are rooted to the spot, enlighten him by stroking down the length of your leg until his eyes fix on the treacherous heel. This educational display will mean the lascivious admirer will have no recourse but to take you... maybe even in his arms.

A GIRL'S SHOES DISCLOSE HER FEELINGS AND WANTS, FOR EXAMPLE:

Cowboy boots say 'Fuck Yeah'

Red-soled stilettos say 'I'm Fucking Expensive'

Bespoke brogues say 'Fuck Off'

Ponyskin stilettos say 'Fancy a Fuck?'

Wellies say 'I Don't Give a Fuck!'

If a suitor is slow to cop-on, then slip into something excruciating and give him a masterclass in Nancy Sinatra and show him 'these boots are made for walking...'.

HOT IN THE CITY — DRESS-DOWN SUMMER

When balmy nights make the sap rise and knickers lower, when scorching days sully your thoughts, you know summer has arrived. Pheromones hang thick in the air like the scent of sex-tangled sheets and seductresses everywhere are on the prowl.

Summer Activities and Wear

Picnics are a quintessential summer activity perfect for al fresco escapades – all you need is a secluded spot, a dishy companion and a hamper laden with goodies. With the right setting and libations, the day should close with a romp in your very own secret garden.

The perfect picnic demands the best ingredients, so do a little research and find out which foods your date loathes and which he adores. Chilled vintage wine, cheap and cheerful bubbles or a jug of Pimm's are synonymous with summer and are perfect to help loosen inhibitions. Fragrant fruits bursting with juices are great for eating and spilling invitingly over lips, fingers and breasts and will certainly awaken hunger in a date who hates to see waste. Finger food is perfect for sharing, and feeding each other is the culinary equivalent of foreplay. Do visit a decent deli for a selection of treats. Great seductive foods include antipasti, bresaola (a wafer-thin cured beef), Ladurée macaroons, strawberries, grapes and bocconcini, to name but a few.

Wearing a dress or skirt that allows for movement is great if you wish to straddle your suitor if a deeper hunger gets the better of you both. Gingerly grind and rock into him while your cunning attire veils anything that would result in a court order for gross public indecency.

If playing croquet, you'll need a playmate or three who display a competitive zeal. Choose clothing that allows you to swing a mallet between your legs and prepare to 'rouquet'. This is the gratuitous act of sending your opponent's balls flying into the bushes. If the game gets dull you can always join him in there.

And don't forget the joys of punting, girls. This traditional British river activity beloved by Oxford and Cambridge chaps can end up being as rude as it sounds. Hire your punt, invite a strapping oarsman to chauffeur you, and lie back and enjoy his exertions. Alternatively, you could take control – some men like a lady to be in command. Wear a soft, sheer dress that catches in the upstream breeze. Make sure it can be dried easily as wetness oft ensues, particularly when on the river.

A body-hugging surf suit, if worn with confidence, can turn a man on enormously. He'll soon be hit by a wave of urgency to prise you out of the ugly garment and warm you with his sporty body.

Even if you are shy, there is something liberating about ripping your clothes off and plunging into an icy lake or river. There is the added excitement that you and your companion could be caught out by a local farmer when skinny-dipping. Don't be surprised if the *eau naturel* look transforms your bathing companion into a freshwater groper.

If you wish to be comfortable (and actually watch the film) at an open-air cinema event, opt for a simple T-shirt and jeans look. If you'd rather go glam, why not evoke Faye Dunaway in *Bonnie and Clyde*; grab yourself your own Warren Beatty, find a lovely secluded area and delight each other with your impressive bodies of work.

Keeping hydrated in sweltering temperatures is important if you don't want to overheat. Always have a bottle of water when travelling and plenty of ice cubes to hand if you and a lover need to cool down after a steamy session.

Finally, a seductress should never be without a fan in summer (no matter how sycophantic he is!).

THE ICE MAIDEN COMETH —
DRESSING FOR WINTER

"I'm as pure as the driven slush."
TALLULAH BANKHEAD

When the outside world proves inhospitable, a seductress must learn to adapt to it, or hibernate with a chosen playmate in her own private winter wonderland.

Warming layers are a girl's best friend when a chill hangs in the air and the outdoors beckons. In a practical sense, the more wrapped up you are, the more you leave to a man's imagination. Winter wardrobes offer tactile and decadent fabrics and all those layers afford a girl the opportunity to gift a boy with a frustratingly slow, teasing strip when she finally disrobes.

For a cool winter look, invoke Julie Christie in *Dr Zhivago*, with a vintage dress, some lace-up boots, a long tailored Russian coat and of course a furry muff. Team your look with a swarthy Cossack and pass lashings of warming vodka decadently from your mouth to his.

If you fancy yourself more as Tilda Swinton's White Witch of Narnia, go for a seriously cool dress and a stole draped over your shoulders. She had legendary powers and if you dress to your full seductive potential, you too should be able to turn men hard with just a glance. Accessorise with a limitless supply of Turkish Delights (recruit in Istanbul).

Vintage or faux fur and no knickers are best reserved for the bolder seductress or purely for indoor misadventures. Ice can lead to falls and a moment of absent-mindedness will see you revealing more in public than ANYONE bargained for. At least the collective burning cheeks will provide some heat.

How To Keep Warm

Picture it: a sweltering wooden cabin packed with glistening Swedish hunks offering to increase your 'circulation' with a gentle birch thrashing. Heaven is a sauna. No wonder you need to jump in ice baths after.

Hot yoga is another great way to stave off the chills of winter and improve your core strength. If you don't fancy a trek to your local studio but still want to get laid on a mat and engage in a series of impossibly sweaty positions, why not invite an athletic lover over?

Winter Pursuits

Ice-skating is a magical winter activity, but it can make maintaining an attractive gait tricky, so why not slip a silk scarf about your man's waist before taking to the rink? You will be able to enjoy turns on the ice without looking like a flailing newborn giraffe and you'll have a good view of your partner. If you trip and go down at least you will land on someone pleasing.

Winter brings out endearingly childlike qualities in people. A trip to a snow-covered park with a boy you like can encourage attractively boisterous behaviour. Nothing says 'I fancy you' like the feeling a girl gets when her bottom is pressed into a chap as they sledge down a perilous hill together.

If that sounds lame perhaps you'd rather make an unusual snowman. For this you will need a laboratory, the DNA of a cool specimen, some sensual genius and a menacing thunderstorm. All going to plan, delighted screams of 'He's alive!' could ensue.

Taking a sleigh ride around Central Park or Prague with a paramour is a romantic thing to do, and thanks to all those blankets covering your laps it can provide the perfect setting for a discreet fumble.

HEAD JOBS — HATS

"Baby take off your dress,
Yes, yes, yes,
You can leave your hat on."
RANDY NEWMAN

In the modern world nude heads tend to be the norm, so a girl in a hat has a sartorial edge and sparks curiosity in those who see her. A great hat should highlight your most attractive features and encourage people to approach you either to offer unsolicited compliments, or to try to jealously thieve the item from your head.

When it comes to choosing the perfect hat, much like selecting a lover, you need to experiment. Finding the right fit is about trial and error. If you want to invest in headwear that crowns your sex appeal a bespoke milliner can help you achieve just the look you want. Hats not only frame a girl's face, but also help her conceal her identity, which proves extremely helpful if she wants to conduct a series of affairs incognito.

The trick to wearing a hat confidently is to choose something that transforms, or accentuates the persona you want to embody – it should tell a story about you. Seductive headgear allows a girl to feel emboldened and a little dramatic without ever being obviously theatrical.

IF THE HAT FITS –
WHAT A HAT SAYS ABOUT A GIRL:

Bowlers bring to mind male commuters from the
1950s, with their stiff upper lips and repressed sexualities;
thankfully they also conjure up Sally Bowles in *Cabaret*,
especially if teamed with a gorgeous basque, briefs
and fishnets.

Top hats are the ultimate in gender-bending hat-chic.
Matched with tails that are altered to your specifications
and a balcony bra just visible beneath, you'll awaken
thrilling confusion in any boy you fancy.

Fedoras evoke prohibition decadence and look perfect
when they sit askew a girl's head as she engages in
forbidden pursuits in a sleazy Dalston or
New Orleans speakeasy.

Panamas are the favoured hats of old money, of playboys in
hot climes and Hemingway-esque men who are desperate
to find someone who can drink them under the table.

Boaters bring out the unruly schoolgirl in a lady.

Mortar boards are perfect if you wish to graduate to the
role of disciplinarian – accessorise with a cane and a
very badly behaved boy.

BELLE (DE JOUR) OF THE BALL —
OCCASION WEAR

Sometimes you will be invited to events where a dress code is mandatory. Some are more palatable than others, and on the whole these codes allow a girl to relax a little as they instantly reduce the number of sartorial choices she can make. Remember, it's not just what you wear, but how you wear it that gets you noticed.

Premières: Don't worry about competing with movie stars: they have a retinue of lackeys tarting them up, but you don't have to be on screen to exude star quality. You can't go wrong with a fitted monochrome cocktail dress, glam heels and a single statement piece of jewellery.

Garden party: Choose something like a light, feminine dress and have a shawl for when it gets colder. Don't forget a pair of sunglasses; squinting does little to woo the boys.

Wedding: If you want to be seductive and don't care about upsetting the bride, be as outrageous as you want. If you are more sisterly, avoid anything white, too short or too low cut. As ever the fit is key, but hold back a little – there is nothing more revolting than an excited vicar.

Balls: These events are traditional but do allow a girl to be more extravagant in her dress. If you want to ensure you have plenty of partners raring to lead you on a merry dance, go for a Jean Harlow look in a satin gown with chic footwear.

Meeting royalty: Wearing an elegant outfit that allows you to curtsey is just good manners – anything too restrictive will make it difficult for you to go down respectfully. If your rear looks outstanding in it, you'll be sure to enrage Pippa and see a Royal flush.

BRA-BARELLA — OUT-OF-THIS-WORLD LINGERIE

"I like a man in my underwear."
YASMINE BLEETH

A girl can't truly reach her full seductive power until she has had a life-changing fitting in a proper lingerie boutique, where an attendant with serious expertise can introduce her to underwear that is fittingly sensuous. Knowing your correct bra-size and investing in seductive lingerie sets helps to add new dimensions to a girl's body and her seductions. Cheap, ill-fitting undies do for breasts what tight plastic shoes do for feet – ruin and hurt them and their erotic endeavours. Invest girls, you may be beautiful on the outside, but you should feel amazing and obscene underneath.

37

Fabulous lingerie has a powerful effect on the wearer and on anyone she allows to glimpse it. A girl with an arse and breasts caressed by silks and lace has increased self-esteem and moves more provocatively than other girls. Remember that when you gift a boy by modelling your magnificent undies, he will find it impossible to have any thoughts other than where his hands may be permitted to wander.

Experiment with lingerie because being daring in your choices will have a deliciously transformative effect on you and help spice things up in the bedroom:

A decadently lacy white set complete with suspenders, even if you are a seasoned seductress, could make you feel like a virginal bride on her wedding night.

A silken, scarlet playsuit could make you feel as though you're Jessica Rabbit – an other-worldly sex-siren pursued by private dicks.

Bras

A Peekaboo-style bra can help tweak an encounter with an ardent nipple lover.

Bandeau bras lend a classical bone structure, giving shape and support to beautiful breasts. Your suitor is bound to appreciate a bra that in the throes of passion also benefits his bone structure.

Balcony bras guarantee that wherever the wearer is she can always provide a breath-taking view.

Push-up bras are especially helpful to a girl with more modest offerings. Make like Florence and the Machine and 'raise them up'.

Padded bras are great for giving a boost to those less well-endowed, but don't over-pad as it could confuse a boy. If nothing else these bras give a spent chap an extra soft place to rest his head.

Strapless bras try their hardest to disprove Newton's law of what goes up must come down. These gravity-defying bras sometimes fail to stand up to the pull of external forces (especially a man's over-eager hands).

Knickers

Perfect briefs are the staple of all girls' lingerie, make sure the ones swathing your sex are made from luxurious material even if you only have them on fleetingly.

G-strings are the salacious sluts of lingerie. These tiny triangles are unabashed and strictly for buttocks that long to walk the tightrope.

Tie-side knickers are properly tantalising, the little ribbon detailing makes them the perfect pair to wear on a boy's birthday before you privately present yourself to be unwrapped by him.

French knickers are best worn while enjoying a restorative café crème in bed, after a satisfyingly exhausting liaison with your paramour.

Stockings and Other Items

Pulling on or taking off a stocking is loaded with licentious significance. As you wantonly sheath the foot, ankle, calf and finally the thigh, the sensation of silk against skin can make a girl feel quite giddy.

Stockings have a universal effect on men that is incredibly HARD to miss. The fabric stimulates a desire in men to stroke with greedy digits the length of a lady's leg from the foot to the soft skin at the thigh. The proximity to the damp inviting lure of a lady's sex is almost overwhelming to them.

If you want to use this sinful garment more pruriently, rather than wearing them yourself, tie one stocking around his cock and balls like an Arab strap, and slip a little silk with your finger into his arse. His member and prostate will swell with ecstasy, and with a little persuasion he will soon be fit to burst.

Suspenders are the star of seduction and stockings are the fluffer. They must be unclipped with reverence and relish before a stocking can be slipped off, and stand attractively and frustratingly between his cock and your... anticipated pleasure.

Waspies are perfect for a girl who likes to be generous with her lingerie as they can be worn over a dress to add a gorgeous silhouette. They don't sting alas, but if he removes it sloppily you can remedy that with a short, sharp, playful slap to his face.

Corsets are rubbish if you prefer breathing to being sexy, but who needs oxygen when these babies make a girl look so fabulously fuckable... The hottest and safest form of autoerotic asphyxiation known to man.

DIAMOND IN THE BUFF —
JEWELLERY

Jewellery was created purely to entrance a girl's inner magpie and to lure a chap's eagle eyes to any part of her body that sparkles prettily. Remember that piling on the bling makes a girl look tacky, so unless you are trying to entice a rapper with a stupid name or a cat burglar, stick to one amazing statement piece or a couple of small accessories.

Diamonds should be worn to stimulate and tease so go for something with a little bit of Gothic detailing like a pair of playful diamond skull earrings. Anything too flashy will make a man wonder if you'll hurt his most sensitive area, his wallet.

Pearls can either be stuffy and elitist, or filthy and suggestive, and a single antique string should be worn with irony because they denote class to a lady, but to a man they say you are posh and dirty. Fingering these delicate white jewels will make a man want to gift you privately with a fresh, glistening string. If he has spent a great deal on your décolletage allow him to admire his magnificent offering before delicately removing some beads with your tongue.

Rings invite men to study a woman's hands and gauge a little information about her style, her romantic status and if she could do him any damage if he accidentally offended her. If a man offers you a more unusual ring, be sure to slip an explorative finger in, he may enjoy it more than he lets on.

A simple gold band on your wedding finger says 'look but don't touch' and yet it is surprising how alluring chaps find other men's wives. If you're not married, don't let that spoil your fun. Commission your very own fabulous and impractical ruby slippers to wear in the boudoir. Click your heels three times, take a deep breath as you gaze upon the creature in front of you and murmur 'lions and tigers and bears, oh my'.

Necklaces instantly highlight sexy collarbones and swan-like necks. However, they are also marvellous if you want to show off your décolletage, and boys can be thankful they have a bona fide excuse to stare at your breasts.

Chandelier earrings lend themselves to a glamorous outfit and frame a girl's face with glinting jewels. Simple diamond studs suggest a girl is more classical, but hoops tend to do a girl's reputation no favours.

Body piercings can be highly arousing to some men, but remember too many can pose logistical issues.

QUEEN BEEHIVE — SEDUCTIVE GROOMING

Good grooming on a girl attracts men on a primal level. Lustrous shiny hair that smells great sends a subconscious message that you are a fertile suitor – even if he doesn't want to make babies with you, he may still be interested in the act that leads to them.

One of the most enduring and important relationships in a girl's life is with her hair stylist; when you find a good one, make sure you keep him/her. An amazing stylist instinctively knows how to give a girl great head and make her ravishing. You need to build up a bond of trust and when you get to that point allow him/her to guide you and take risks – comfort zones are for the sexually sedentary.

Remember that being a slave to the hairdresser is expensive, time-consuming and could leave you bald. Save expert styling for a seduction you are really serious about. The more precious you are about your hair, the less sexy you will be to a boy, because you will be too focused on him messing up your do.

To Dye For

Gentlemen, it is said, prefer blondes and Marilyn Monroe and Cameron Diaz certainly make an argument in favour of switching to platinum. Blonde hair screams youth, virginity and paradoxically Playboy bunnies, which are a few of men's favourite things.

Raven-haired beauties suggest a more experienced, exotic seductress, like Monica Bellucci or Linda Fiorentino, who will make men yearn for certain dark acts.

Flame-headed sirens seem to promise fiery sexual high-jinks and attract men who want to tame them. Julianne Moore and Joséphine de la Baume scream sensual glamour – what man hasn't wanted the 'red carpet' treatment?

It takes a strong woman to take clippers to her tresses and a stronger man still to embrace the look – for some reason, men have no problem with a shaven pussy, but balk at a silky smooth cranium. You might not be Natalie Portman, who proved that bald can be sexy, but if you have a well-shaped head, piercing eyes and small ears you may win a boy round to this look!

With weaves, you need to see an expert! Human hair is preferable to synthetics and having them sewn in is classier than opting for the glued approach. There's nothing seductive about a tell-tale trail of locks left in your wake. Think Kelly Rowland or Jennifer Hudson for a look that is fierce.

The Bush

A lady needs to be as confident about her do-below as the one she has on her head. Only ever solicit a man's advice on your intimate styling if you feel it will improve his lip servicing, because you have to live with it. Bear in mind a full-on bush is old school and will appeal more to a mature man. A Hollywood will appeal to any boy with an interest in pornos, but could make you feel uncomfortably regressive.

Manicures

Obscenely long, fake talons with scenes of dolphins and palm trees arouse a fear of being punctured in men, and show him a lady who has been adversely affected by nail-polish fumes. Perfect nails are subtly maintained, a decent length and used as tools to stroke a lover, rather than for scratching your name into his chest.

Oral Hygiene

Coating your lips with gorgeous lipstick will be pointless if you haven't dedicated time to brushing, flossing, gargling and spitting. Your mouth should always be fresh and inviting if you want to score. The last part of this regime could prove a useful warm-up for later shenanigans.

Scent

Fragrance is so important when attracting the opposite sex – just as animals size each other up with smell, so too do humans. The better you smell, the closer a guy will want to get to you. A lot of women choose one scent that they stick to, without regarding whether it complements the smell of their skin. Perfume should never mask your natural fragrance but rather enhance it. A trip to a perfumery will help you get to know what is right for you. Choose two scents – one for day and one for evening – which should contrast slightly, but both should be as alluring and identifiable as you are.

Spritz perfume anywhere you yearn to be kissed – and I mean anywhere.

Scent is crucial to sexual chemistry and if you can't stand the smell of a guy, no matter how hot he is, your pairing is doomed to fail.

CHAPTER THREE

24-hour party people

"*Going so soon? Why, I wouldn't hear of it. My little party's only just starting.*"

WICKED WITCH OF THE WEST

When it comes to parties, you never know who will turn up. Even if you are hosting, there is always a possibility that an attractive gatecrasher could wreak havoc upon your hormones. Remember that a truly 'sexy party' isn't about burning the candle at both ends, but more about how you use the molten wax.

INVITATIONS — AN OFFER THEY CAN'T REFUSE

Shoving a horse's head complete with party details into a boy's bed will certainly get his attention, but if you actually want him to show up, tell him so. If you want a boy to feel extra special, let him know that if he were absent the party would be only half as fun.

If your occasion is exclusive, you must make it obvious that what you are offering is not open to just everyone. Highlight the strict entrance policy for your private affair... all being well he'll lap up such an invite.

To make your party attractive to a potential lover, hint at the treats you have in store. The best invitations let the recipient know how much better a night would go if they were actively involved in it. If his idea of enticement equals promises of free beer and limitless PlayStation, ask to see his ID – if he is a teenager send him back to his mum's, if he's a grown man send him to Coventry.

When addressing your invitee, include a little information to prepare him for what's to come:

✳ If it's a drinks party, let him know if he needs to bring a bottle. To whet his appetite you could hint at a nightcap you'd like to give him that's twice as intoxicating.

✳ Remember, dress codes can be intimidating and put people off an event. Most men prefer dress-down affairs, so oblige if you are feeling generous.

✳ Parties can spill over into the wee hours and if you have work the next day, you may not be up for an all-nighter. Let him know if there are any time restrictions for your affair. Stopwatches at the ready aren't very romantic, but at least your party will end with a bang.

The style of your invitation is dependent on the type of party you are having. Expensive, heavy paper embossed with details is for a conservative do, but an event detailed on exotic underwear will let him know your party will be rather unorthodox. Alternatively an invite can be as simple as making suggestive eye contact, or opening up your body language to show you are happy to be approached.

To be the hostess with the mostess, you must stay relaxed and actually enjoy the build-up to your party. Stress puts everyone on edge and does little to enhance a girl's charms. A girl who is welcoming and in control without ever being domineering makes an attractive hostess to whom guests will naturally gravitate.

If you have invited a man who you can't figure out, make sure to also invite some other men you know fancy you. It will help you work out how interested he is in you, because men's true intentions always shine through when they see they have competition.

Catering to guests' needs is vital if you want them to be relaxed and happy, but how far are you willing to go? If you have a guest you know is shy help him to come out of his shell, but do remember it's the quiet ones you have to watch.

Be generous – if it's a big do, don't hog all the available bachelors, but help single girls to mingle. A munificent lady is an attractive force to her friends and lovers.

Enure that guests' thirsts are quenched and their hungers catered to, but remember some people have insatiable appetites; don't be shocked if you get eaten out... of house and home.

Party games can either be cringe-worthy or help break the ice. Tequila Twister is silly and offers an excuse to touch someone you fancy, but remember the more shots you do, the quicker things will descend into debauchery.

When the last of your guests has passed out you can turn on your heels, making your way through the deluge of bottles, clothing, bodies and licentious debris to your boudoir, where your plus one awaits. No party is complete without a select after-party.

GUEST TO IMPRESS — WOWING HOSTS

When responding to an invite, remember timing is key and the more arrogant he is, the longer you need to make him wait.

Taking a gift for your host shows you are an appreciative guest, so choose something that will reflect the occasion and the recipient's tastes (if his are deviant perhaps gift him in private).

There is nothing more awkward than being stuck with someone at a party who is monosyllabic. The broader your passions, the more likely people will engage with you. Avoid religion or politics unless you find yourself chatting with a sexy MP. The occasional heated 'mass debate' is enlivening, unless it's with a Conservative, which is a shameful transgression.

Never turn up to a party draped in a beautiful man unless you have been permitted a plus one, or if the host is an ex you want to make jealous. If you arrive with a partner with whom you have a secure bond it is fine to gently flirt with other men. He'll enjoy the attention other men give you as it will heighten his pride that he is yours.

If you are single and ready to mingle, indulge your wandering eye and peruse male guests at your leisure. You are beholden to no one and can have fun at your own pace. By the end of the night, you might have a new friend who may prove to have appealing benefits.

Try to show a little restraint at least when it comes to booze. Tipsy is fine, but a woman who morphs into a drunken nightmare and swings knickerless from antique chandeliers or other women's husbands will soon be ejected.

If your host looks like he needs de-stressing, why not offer a helping hand to lighten his load – thoughtful actions are always an attractive quality.

Never be the first to arrive or the last to leave unless it is expressly requested and you are both unable to hold out any longer.

SOCIAL ROULETTE: THE DANGERS AND DELIGHTS OF MEET AND GREETS

If you spy someone who gives you a funny feeling in your undercarriage and you want to know more, approach your host and ask for insider information or an introduction. Alternatively approach them yourself, because most men would be flattered by the attentions of a beautiful girl.

A warm, genuine smile is important when you want to show interest in a boy. Smiling invites a guy to focus on your lips, and the longer his gaze is focused there you'll find the greater his interest in kissing you.

If you meet someone who makes you want to tear his clothes off, do show some decorum by introducing yourself with a handshake instead and save more forward advances for later. A firm grip shows spunk, which men find sexy in a lady.

Flaccid hands are vile and a pumping shake doesn't so much say 'glad to meet you' as 'I work on a dairy farm' which is a massive turn-off, unless he is a farmer.

A peck to the cheek, especially on the continent, is a fairly usual greeting. The only tricky element is how many times say friendly and how many times before it is considered foreplay?

A good trick when at a party rammed with gorgeous specimens is to choose three utterly different men to talk to. Variety is the spice of lust and adding flavour to your night will see your tastes become more adventurous. Don't play it safe.

Eye Spy: Covert Glances

There is something delicious about the initial moment you catch a stranger's eye and palpable sparks fly between you. It can be agonising waiting for someone to make the first move, all the while imagining the feel of their body, the sharpness of their brain or the size of their bank account.

As noted earlier in the book, girls with smoky come-to-bed eyes prove irresistible to boys. Thick lashes of mascara, dark eyeshadow and accentuating eye-shape with liner will help make your peeps smoulder.

Glasses appeal to men with naughty librarian fantasies who see their removal as a sexy visual disrobing. If a girl unpinned her hair at the same time he'd be won over.

EYE WANT TO SEDUCE YOU

Flirting using your eyes opens up a world of dialogue, which reveals and conceals your sexual intentions simultaneously. The visual signals you offer a suitor should suggest something more is being offered to him than meets the eye, and to unearth it he must ultimately look deeper.

The more attracted you are to a man, the more your arousal will show in your eyes. It is no accident that when we fancy someone our pupils dilate exactly as they would during sexual intercourse. Honing your visual flirting skills helps when spotting the difference between a man who is aroused by you and a man with an appetite for MDMA.

Looking at a man's mouth for a period signals that you would like to kiss him, but staring will make him paranoid he has food in his teeth or a sore on his lip.

DIFFERENT GAZES

If you want to make a boy feel more masculine, the coquettish look can't be rivalled, think Carey Mulligan in *Shame* for this unthreatening but teasing look. Tilt your head towards your suitor and look up at him through your lashes while flashing a wry smile.

If you are not directly facing a potential suitor, play eyed-and-seek and intermittently turn your gaze to meet his. Hold it for a few seconds and smile mischievously as you look away. Repeat, each time meeting his eyes for a little longer.

If wink murder is more your thing, saucily bat your eyelids sparingly at a man. It's flirty, it's silly and if played right can lead to unspeakable acts in the ballroom.

To add power to your gazes think of what you want your eyes to say as you look at a chap and repeat that line over in your head as you cast a look his way:

Gentle: 'Eye want to get to know you better.'

Hardcore: 'By the time Eye am finished with you, you won't be able to see straight.'

PRACTISE YOUR LOOK

Eye contact that is too drawn out or intense won't read so much 'You and me, it's on', but more 'I have a knife, run'. You may think you have your seductive gaze locked down, but I would recommend you test it out in a mirror. You may feel stupid doing this, but better to practise than go out and find that the hot look you have been giving guys verges on crazed.

Tongue Twisting

First impressions are formed quickly so when you are talking to someone new make sure that what you say is worth hearing and your delivery is attractive and audible. If you initiate an interaction with someone, it is up to you to make sure you open with something engaging.

People respond best to someone who is genuinely interested in them, interesting and good company. Remember, bitching about people or offloading are big no-nos and aren't even appealing to therapists, who at least know it will come to an end and they will get paid.

Conversation is the slowest form of human expression, so always have an opening line to speed up the pace:

'*Can I buy you a drink?*' Alcohol and a beautiful woman, he will be beside himself.

'*Hi stranger... how about we get familiar?*' The forward approach can help lead things in the right direction.

'*Let's get you out of those wet clothes.*' When he looks confused, pour some water on him.

Ask leading and open questions to find out what you would like to know about him, as these give you clues as to how to continue. Open questions demand explanations – not just a simple 'yes' or 'no':

'*I am conducting a survey on people's biggest fantasies and I was keen to know what yours is?*' is cheeky and unusual and might garner you an intriguing response.

Flex your intellectual muscles without fear because contrary to popular belief most men like a woman who can teach them a thing or two. A woman should only ever dumb down if she thinks it will be beneficial.

Holding court is fine, but remember to be inclusive even if you don't usually like sharing – generosity is an attractive quality in all areas of a girl's character. Do you have similar interests? Talking to someone can unearth passions that you both share which help to strengthen your initial connections. Carpet-bombing a guy with your life story can be a devastating error and will see most men running for safety.

Whispering is impolite so make sure that what you are saying is seriously rude to make all those disapproving looks warranted. If you don't wish to offend others, why not place your hand on the nape of his neck and pull him close as though you are about to kiss his cheek before whispering your very private yearnings? Finish by kissing his ear, as they are very sensitive and more so after a lust-filled exchange.

Listening attentively to a man will allow him to believe he has your undivided attention and make him feel special. A nod or laugh at appropriate moments are physical affirmations to show you are listening to what a man is saying. Even if you are bored rigid and only want his body, at least give the impression that you are interested.

Try to share equally with a man you are conversing with, meaning to never give away more than he does – it allows you to have an even level of mystique.

TOUCHING HIS FUNNY BONE — HUMOUR'S ALLURE

A refined lady walks into a chemist's and approaches the counter:
'I'd like three AA batteries please.'
The pharmacist smiles, beckons her with his finger and says,
'Of course, Madam. Come this way.'
The lady shoots him a look of incredulity and says
'If I could cum that way I wouldn't need these.'

Without humour serious seduction would be impossible – it increases your pulling power ten-fold by showing emotional and social intelligence, and reveals to a man that he can enjoy you on more than one level. Being funny lends a magnetic sexual power to those who know how to use it, how else would Woody Allen ever get laid?

Humour requires two fundamental skills – timing and delivery. A man or a woman who knows when and how to deliver the goods will prove utterly irresistible to his or her audience.

Pushing the boundaries is just as important when bantering as it is in physical seduction. So you need to offer him something to really get his laughing gear around.

It is important that a lady knows how to deal with hecklers. Gain control by fixing him with a confident but sympathetic look, saying 'Men should be obscene and not heard'. If that doesn't work, you could always try another gag on him. I find satsumas work beautifully.

An excellent example of how humour can seduce comes from a personal ad that commanded several thousand eager responses: 'Lady Doctor likes laughing in bed.' What was its appeal? She was alluringly economic with words – letting suitors know simply she had a brain, she was fun, and up for it.

It is handy to use humour as a foil for unveiling a truth safely – if you fancy someone, you can put it out there and gauge his interest without having to lose face. Humour affords a girl the opportunity to tease a boy – a little light ribbing, as any girl knows, can be very pleasurable, but refrain from taking the joke too far because no one likes to feel ridiculed.

If you find yourself being laughed into bed, lucky you! I sincerely hope it's the best 'stand up' you have encountered.

BODY OF EVIDENCE — SPEAKING IN TONGUES

"I speak two languages: body and English."
MAE WEST

Being bilingual is essential to making sure he trips deliciously on your tongue.

Sign Language

Your body is continuously in a state of narrative so you need to be in tune with it to make sure nothing gets lost in translation and nothing is disclosed that you'd rather remained private. You must learn to use your body to create the right level of intimacy with a boy; the closer you get, the fewer barriers he will have to protect himself from your wicked ways.

It's interesting to note that the deaf, whose actions truly speak louder than words, use the most potent sign language of all. Everything they sign is economical and all intentions are indicated explicitly and swiftly. If only hearing-people could communicate as directly, seductions would be a lot easier.

Hands do the majority of work when we talk with our bodies, but beware flailing gesticulations, which can make you appear as though you're signalling a plane into land. Hand movements can help to animate a story, so you need touch to help get your real point across. Brushing your fingers over a boy's arm affirms subtle interest and allows gentle contact, whereas stroking his leg signifies that you are keen for more intimacy. If he is a sportsman, you can use a 'legitimate' sporting interest to explore his thighs further.

When attracted to someone, girls naturally turn their

bodies to face a chap – simply direct yours accordingly. It isn't tricky unless there are multiple men to choose from. If you are sitting next to a guy you have the hots for, cross your legs so the top one points in his direction to hint you are keen and gently brush it against his leg to get his attention. When uncrossing your legs avoid flashing a boy your gusset, no matter how badly you want his attention.

You could remove something from his person as an excuse to touch him, such as a bit of fluff from his jacket, or if you prefer the more direct approach, be more hands-on. If you want his eyes on your body, try absent-mindedly loosening a couple of buttons on your blouse, before stroking the exposed skin gently with the tips of your fingers as you fix him with a naughty gaze.

A dark, rouge-stained mouth parted ever so slightly as you gaze lustfully at a suitor will make a man do more than read your lips, he will be keen to fill in the gaps as well!

Resting your head in a man's lap is best reserved for someone you know a bit better and wish to indulge in a more intimate language with. Never encroach on a man's personal space – take your time to get closer, getting up in his grill only works if you are Missy Elliot.

If an unpleasant space-invader is ruining your atmosphere with his unwanted proximity, a display of defensive body language (something hard of yours connecting with something soft of his) will tell him that he is 'over and out'.

Mirroring the movements of someone you are attracted to relays a subconscious message to them that you are compatible and in tune. But only ever repeat everything their body communicates if you are playing an X-rated version of Simon Says.

✳ Holding a man's hands can suggest you want to bring him into your confidence or that you wish to lead him astray.

✳ Caressing a boy's back can be done surreptitiously if you don't want others to see your physical connection. Sometimes contact is more exciting if it is furtive.

✳ A hug is the perfect request of the secret pervert, allowing you to subtly press yourself to a man's body. From there you can negotiate more revealing explorations of his body.

✳ Arm flexion – if a man flexes his bicep at you, try to resist the urge to be sick. If he does it in bed, or worse, kisses it while engaged in a sexual act strongly suggest he and his love muscle get a room.

✳ Face to face is a very charged position whether vertical or horizontal.

✳ Tapping of fingers on a beer bottle can show nervous energy or pent-up sexual energy. If they deep throat the bottle, you may find you are with Madonna.

✳ Buttock patting is intensely annoying and patronising, and for some women who have fraught relationships with their bums, a man highlighting it with a slap may well deserve one in return – in the face. If you want to slap a man's bum try to resist, it screams 'drunk hen'. A subtle stroke is much better.

Deportment

Walking about with books on your head should be strictly reserved for role-play, you as a doe-eyed finishing school debutante and he the cruel, commanding master. Accessorise with an Austrian accent, a cane and an inviting bottom.

CHAPTER FOUR

Eating out

"Hunger can explain many acts.
The most lustful acts are carried
out to satisfy it."

M. GORKY

Food is the perfect prop for the sensual being. It's not merely a fuel source, but an essential component in awakening every conceivable hunger. The food you choose and the manner in which you consume it relates to a companion how sophisticated or adventurous your personal and sexual tastes are.

A good appetite is an attractive quality in a woman. Being orally delighted is far more appetising to a man than a woman who puts all her energies into pushing food around her plate. Inhaling food like a hoover might be advantageous on a humiliating TV game show, but it will be detrimental to strengthening romantic bonds with a boy – nothing kills passion quite like acid reflux.

When on a date, it shows a certain class and generosity of character to order something you are able to share with your dining companion. If he has a crustacean allergy ordering a crab dish could, if shared unawares, have an unfortunate result. Sharing allows you the opportunity to literally feed a lover, which by its very nature is sexy, and it demonstrates that you are not selfish which will indicate to a boy your boudoir behaviour.

Always be open to sampling new things. There is a parallel between experimenting with men and restaurants; the more adventurous you are the more sophisticated your palette becomes and you soon work out the things that do not appeal to you.

If you don't know what something is on a menu (which increases in likelihood the more expensive the restaurant), ask. You wouldn't put just any old thing in your mouth romantically speaking and when dining you should try to be equally informed. Also, there is nothing wrong with pointing at something on a menu if you are unable to pronounce it, though it can be cute to attempt to as it shows you are not afraid of getting things wrong. A girl who strives to be perfect at all times is exhausting.

Remember eating out should be fun in every sense. The very fact you don't have to cook should relax you instantly, but the choice of restaurant is key if you and a date want things to stay that way. Fashionable restaurants largely attract pretentious types and snobbish waiting staff who can be amusing and give you and a date plenty to talk about; but if unbroken intimacy and delicious food are what you want, go for a relatively unknown gem.

If you find a foreign body in your food that doesn't have a passport, a rich accent and blush-inducing customs, sensitively attract the attention of your waiter and alert him to the intruder. Never make a massive scene over such things because they can be easily remedied and waiters will be more willing to tend to your needs if you treat them with courtesy. Only incredibly classless and unpleasant people are rude to staff, it is not seductive to look down on people unless literally and while engaged in an intimate moment. Rudeness in a dining companion is a total turn-off and encourages kitchen staff to lace your dish with unpleasant extras.

Flirting with restaurant staff leads to a more attentive service. Remember, they're trying to increase what they take home at the end of a shift, so if you want to pursue it further make sure they are a more enticing option than your companion. How gratuitous should your gratuity be?

Napkins are not just for spillages but also to thwart strangers' glances as your companion's avaricious hands arouse a hidden appetite beneath. Mauling each other on the table (or under it) is unfair to other diners who may not be as lucky. Go to the powder room instead. A frenetic fuck will encourage new-found appetites.

ORAL FIXATION — SPECIAL MEALS

Putting effort into anything you offer orally is disarming, especially if you want a boy to eat out of your palm. Remember that what you eat directly affects the way you taste – if your ingredients are fresh and fragrant, you'll discover that your most intimate areas and those of a lover will be the more delicious.

Doing your prep early gives you more time to relax before your dinner date, so get all the tricky bits out of the way asap. Don't slave over a hot stove all day unless you like that sort of thing. Cooking needn't be an awful experience so focus on the positives, because if you're having fun making a meal it will show through satisfyingly in the finished product.

Cooking allows a girl to be creative and can be extremely cathartic not to mention a wonderful stimulator of multiple senses. If you feel a little stressed, why not make some fresh bread to go with dinner? Dough takes energy to work, but it will leave you a lot more relaxed and your guest will be delighted to be met by the alluring aroma of baking.

For inspiration consult the Internet or a trusted cookery book, and although the title may convince you otherwise, don't look for tips by watching *The Cook, The Thief, His Wife & Her Lover* unless you need help with post-meal activities.

If you feel your date could spill over into something sexier why not offer your boy things that will make him even tastier:

❋ *Chilli:* Improves the taste of intimate areas, though only when ingested. Perfect if you want a hot encounter, but wash your hands thoroughly or his loins will be agonisingly aflame.

❋ *Gold:* You can get wafer-thin slivers of edible gold, which can be added to any food to add attractiveness and put lead in a lover's pencil. The Mayans used gold leaf as a natural Viagra and its properties are legendary.

✳ *Vanilla:* These fragrant pods infuse anything you put them in with a sensual sweetness – this includes men.

✳ *Pomegranates:* A dark delicacy of the gods connected to lust, their bejewelled insides burst with rich juices. Serve sliced in half and squeezed temptingly over parts of your body.

When creating a seductive dining ambience, consider how you want your guest to feel and how intimate you want things to be. If you have prepared a Japanese meal, for example, it's a nice touch to serve it traditionally and sit on cushions on the floor to eat – this removes the obstacle of a table and breaks down physical boundaries. Serving sushi on your body is hazardous as you will need to leave the door on the latch, and you may find your feast is ruined by an intrusive neighbour.

Having candles strategically placed around the dining area adds to the intimacy, but avoid scented ones as they could overpower the seductive aromas coming from the kitchen.

Ensure that your wine is given plenty of time to breathe or chill before your date arrives and make sure you follow suit.

If you want some mood music, keep the volume low and play songs that have a subtle subtext of where you'd like the night to go. Avoid any artists who might ruin either of your appetites, like Bananarama.

Brush up on your Nigellaisms, the queen of food-related filth knows that peppering food talk with suggestive phrases will make a man drool. For example:

'Is my rump tender enough for you?'
'Now tell me, are you a breast or a leg man?'
'Would you like more juice on your meat?'
'Can I interest you in a creamy horn puff?'

Always be ready to offer your guest more because a growing boy won't be able to resist and if the night goes how you want, he will need all his strength.

SLIPPERY WHEN WET —
TROUBLESOME FOOD

Things we put in our mouths can occasionally prove tricky because of their size, shape, or texture. Unwieldy and slippery offerings take on lives of their own, and sometimes miss our mouths entirely, leaving telltale stains on a lady's face or finery. You must become a culinary Goldilocks recognising what you can handle with seductive oral finesse – is it simply too big, too hard and what is just right?

You would be wise to avoid anything that is too oily, too flaky, too smelly or aesthetically horrifying when selecting either food or lovers. If a man offers you any part of himself that falls into these categories, it is advisable to refuse on the grounds of having (and wanting a) good taste.

If you are offered a delicacy that looks delish but tastes rank, try not to spit it out in disgust instantly. Excuse yourself and dispose of the unwanted mouthful in the lavatory. It saves hurting anyone's feelings and you retain your charming demeanour. If he attempts to give you another helping he is clearly the worst sort of feeder!

Delicious as garlic is, it is a terrible foe of seduction. A woman who reeks as badly as a French cliché will prove upsettingly easy to turn down if she asks a man to 'voulez-vous coucher avec moi ce soir?'

Eating soup on a date is just tempting fate. Avoid it, as slurping is gross and there are better hot accidents to be had.

Pasta and noodles are scrumptious, but are messy to eat seductively and at worst can make a girl look like a baby bird with a mouth full of worms. If you can twirl and suck artfully you will find your host will be most impressed by your gifts.

SILVER-TONGUED SERVICE —
FORMAL DINING

Michelin-starred establishments can be intimidating temples with god-like chefs attracting pretentious patrons with groaning wallets who go just to be fashionable. This clientele prefer sneering loudly into their phones and studiously ignoring bored companions to actually eating. Thankfully such things don't deter girls who understand the lure of new sensory pleasures and when matched with a delectable companion you can help put the fine back into dining.

For all their theatrics these restaurants excel in a passion for broadening people's palates, and what girl could resist dishes that a chef has poured (not literally, it would contravene hygiene laws) blood, sweat and tears into?

If you are eating with a suitor, these tricks to get his juices flowing will happily help aid seduction as well as digestion:

✳ Boys like a girl who can take her time when it comes to pleasurable experiences, so pace yourself, eating and fucking are two things you should never finish too quickly.

✳ Even if you think a boy has expressed how much it would turn him on to see you 'masticate', it's still advisable to take bite-size mouthfuls and savour your food, because chances are you misheard him.

✳ Taking pleasure in your food is a big turn-on, whereas someone who is all picky comes across as joyless and difficult.

✳ Punctuate mouthfuls with occasional understated groans of pleasure to instantly make a man imagine how closely they match the sounds you make in the boudoir.

✳ Foods often sound rude and lend themselves to playful innuendos such as 'Please, describe your tenderloin to me'.

✳ Order foods that can be eaten sensually (and act as aphrodisiacs), such as asparagus tips or oysters.

✳ If food leaves you with juice around your mouth, do not wipe it away, but lick. Subconsciously lips make men think of girl's pussies and this act can be gently arousing to him.

GOLD FINGER — HAVING THE MIDAS TOUCH WITH CANAPÉS

Canapés often come before you are ready for them, are rarely satisfying and leave just when you need them most, rather like a disappointing sexual encounter. Position yourself in the line of the waiters and remember, as with lovers, the more appreciative you are, the more regularly they will come to you.

Smears of grease decorating your lips won't make a man want to kiss you, so choose morsels that can be easily popped into your mouth without disturbing your look. Your selections are important when drawing the right sort of attention to your mouth – choose, for example, asparagus, which is delicious and suggestively phallic. Only savour the supple tip, as going lower will leave you with a mouth of woody shaft that even Linda Lovelace would have refused.

Patisserie oozing with cream is a daring choice and must be devoured quickly, because nibbling leads to accidents. Make sure you have a napkin to hand; fingers smeared with chocolate will attract admiring attention only from deviant guests.

If a man offers you oysters, he is likely feeling libidinous and you can be certain he will enjoy watching as you swallow. Go for a smaller one and enjoy the sensation of its slippery descent.

Mini-burgers are instantly gratifying and help to soak up booze, but dainty finger food they ain't. If you don't mind butching-up, you'll be able to eat them with dignity and attract admiration from a boy who likes a girl who enjoys her meat. A firm grip is essential.

If you want to appear more femme then choose cocktail sausages, which are perfectly easy to eat seductively and prove that size doesn't matter. Sadly a honey and mustard marinade can only do so much to improve a gentleman's shortcomings.

Vol-au-vents are impossibly messy, and when it comes to your mouth anything stuck in the 80s should not be stuck in your gob... sorry David Hasselhoff.

VINCENT PRICE — TAKING THE HORROR OUT OF PAYING

A battle of wills when it comes to paying can start by feeling like foreplay and end in a full-on battle of the sexes, so why not keep the peace by telling him he can remunerate you in other ways if he wishes.

If a restaurant is heaving, getting a waiter to bring you the bill can take time, which is frustrating if you are both keen to work off some of those calories with an energetic clinch. Relax and remind yourself that the longer the build-up, the greater the release will be. Catch the waiter's eye, but remember they are often juggling a few things at once. The more potent your gaze the more likely the ensuing sound of smashing plates. Snapping your fingers like a surly queen from the Middle Ages will see you are swiftly ignored and waiting even longer.

If the dinner was your suggestion, then you should be prepared to pay, or at the very least give every indication that you will. It's shocking how many women automatically assume a man will pay, so prove an exception because boys are disarmed by demonstrations of independence.

'Going Dutch' is not a hedonistic act hailing from the red light district of Amsterdam, though why let that stop you suggesting one after you have both contributed toward the bill?

If your companion orders excessive amounts of rich foods and vintage wines while you have had only a salad, it is only fair he foots most of the bill. If he protests, do make sure that any 'fuck' he had hoped for is swiftly followed by an 'off'.

If you earn more than him choose a restaurant where he will not feel intimidated or inadequate, because unfortunately those feelings can carry into the bedroom.

Twelve per cent is average when tipping, but if the waiter is cute and your dining companion left a bad taste in your mouth you could bump it up by adding your number too. It's called the service industry for a reason.

LONE HUNTER — EATING EN SOL

There is something provocative about a girl eating alone. It is a remarkably empowering act and a powerful visual, and attracts far more admiring attention than you might think. Be confident and it will work to your advantage, because tasty strangers are more likely to approach you in such a moment than if you were eating with friends.

If you are all Greta Garbo and 'vant to be alone', there is something decadent about treating yourself to a restaurant meal, so enjoy the sensation of eating without having to share or feel you have to behave demurely.

For an instant ego boost, solo dining is perfect – you are guaranteed increased service from waiters who enjoy flattering and flirting with a pretty girl. Who cares if they are trying to increase their tip or genuinely see it as a perk of the job, as long as your experience is heightened by the attention? You never know what could happen or whom you might meet, your meal could start with something simple and end with someone complex.

KEEPING YOUR SPIRITS UP

Drinking is the quickest and most socially acceptable way to publicly add lubrication to your seductive activities. It allows lovers to lower their guards, steady their nerves and forget their inhibitions, which is advantageous if you want to know someone more intimately. But impaired judgement can be an unfortunate side effect of drinking. Beware the altering effects of spirits – one too many and you'll wake with the fear, five too many and you can throw someone horrifying into the bargain.

Excessive alcohol can also inhibit an otherwise perfect specimen's performance. Still, there is nothing quite like the half-cut light of a new day for transforming brewer's droop into a mutually restorative morning glory. Some people swallow raw eggs to cure their hangover – sex is much more enjoyable.

Abstinence makes drinkers louder and duller. If you are sober because you are the designated driver or you just don't drink, you shouldn't have to suffer. Thankfully being alert allows you to see people in their truest colours and, if you have no scruples, to take advantage of vulnerable men.

If a boy is being discourteous and trying to pressure you to drink, shut him up by explaining that 'even booze won't help make you attractive to me'. That should sober him up.

If invited to a wine tasting, note that these are refined affairs where swilling wine around your mouth is customary rather than taking large swigs. Decent wine should be savoured and the depth of its bouquet relished. Don't forget that this is the one place a man won't take it personally if you spit.

When at a restaurant you may be looking for something aged, full-bodied and rich, or light, young and complex to go with your meal, but remember sommeliers can only help you with your wine selection.

Champagne is the traditional drink of celebration and seduction. Combine the two and it proves even more delicious.

Lastly girls, when drinking you should always retain sufficient self-awareness and control to ensure you never do or say anything that you could not back up when sober.

CHAPTER FIVE

Getting about

"*I like to go fast... sometimes in cars.*"

LARA FLYNN BOYLE

Imagine how much more enjoyable journeys could be, and how road rage would be reduced if we used vehicles to transport ourselves to our destinations by way of seductive and erotic detours.

The lure of driving for a girl is not about being a poseur behind the wheel, but about instant freedom and the adventure that cars afford. There is something extremely attractive about stealing out to your ride in the wee hours with a personable companion before speeding off on a nocturnal jaunt and seeing where it leads you.

Car manufacturers love to push the fallacy that if you drive a hot car, the more sexually in demand you will be. If that were true Ferrari drivers would either be absent from the roads most of the time or creaking along due to the excessive amounts of libidinous passengers. Even if your wheels are affixed to a beloved old banger, as long as it goes from A to B and has a comfortable and clean interior with easily adjustable seats, you are in possession of something potentially seductive.

Boys love gadgets, though be warned that these can become competition for your attention. If you want a boy to focus on you then simple features in a car prove to be much more beneficial to a girl – for example, the humble rear-view mirror is perfect for touch-ups when stationary, and especially for giving a tempting backseat companion the eye when you feel the need to move things along.

Why not drive your boy to a picturesque spot, open up the sunroof and stand, enjoying the view as your companion drives you wild below?

HOW TO DRIVE SEDUCTIVELY

A girl should always be confident, focused and clear about the direction she is heading in. Indecision in driving and in romance can be dangerous for you and irritating to others. Never lose your temper on the roads, it doesn't solve anything and can make your driving unattractively aggressive. Show courtesy to other drivers even if they do not afford you the same manners as it will make you a pleasure to drive with.

A girl who drives well is a massive turn-on to boys, especially if she handles a stick shift expertly which allows her the opportunity to accidentally brush her passenger's knee. If you can make your passenger feel that he is in good hands, you not only stick one finger up to misogynists, but you will also find a boy will let you take charge in other fast activities.

If you fear becoming a gorgeous taxi-service, deliberately take your lover out on a white-knuckle ride. Sidle onto the pavement, steer too close to verges and apply mascara at crucially hazardous moments. You'll never be the designated driver again!

Remember to rest between exhausting rides – this is equally good advice when on long journeys.

If your passenger is proving seriously distracting, pull into a lay-by and do whatever you need to clear your corrupted mind, but do be aware that transport police might be watching.

Before taking to the road, remember the golden rule of the seduction highway code: if you wouldn't let a man ride in your car, you should never permit him anywhere else.

RIDING TANDEM — THE JOY OF CYCLING

Racing about on a warm summer's day astride your two-wheeler lends a certain wanton flush to a girl, especially when the sun is caressing your face and a cooling breeze tickles tenderly around your saddle. If you don't own a bike, don't fret; many cities have some sort of communal bike-hire system available. You can merrily pick one up on a street corner, take it for a joyous spin and then deposit it at a designated point without any sense of commitment or guilt. If only all random pick-ups were as easy.

The benefits of cycling are huge, it's good for the environment, great for your figure and offers up plenty of opportunities for flirting with other free-wheelers.

Wearing Lycra only works if you are super body-confident as it is as unforgivably clingy as a neurotic boyfriend. Wearing a summer dress or jeans allows for freer movement, but dresses are preferable if you fancy treating a courier to an accidental knicker flash. Few girls can make a cycling helmet seductive, however who cares if they help to protect you from injury – you can up your sexy credentials elsewhere.

Cycling Essentials

If you are going on a long ride, padded pants are an option, but there is a cost to avoiding saddle-soreness, as these bottoms will make you walk as though you are wearing a nappy.

A firm grip around the handlebars is essential for manoeuvring your ride... After Movember get him to shave it off, the porn-star plumber look is passé.

Hand signals need to be blatant and made in good time. Left, right, up a bit, they are essential for safe cycling and can also be adopted in the bedroom if you need a boy to follow your direction.

Chains can slip or break so always make sure yours are secure and you know how to put them back on. You don't want him escaping before you've finished with him.

Never go on a ride without making sure the tyres are properly inflated. A girl knows that certain things demand a good pump to make sure they are in serviceable condition.

WHAT YOUR BIKE SAYS ABOUT YOU:

Mountain Bike: Likes rides on any terrain.

Rally Racer: Catch me if you can.

Tandem: Likes to watch as you let him do all the work.

Dutch Bike: How dare you!

Penny Farthing: Not adverse to a Prince Albert.

Adult Tricycle: Super kinky and frankly rather disturbing.

HORSE PLAY — RULING YOUR STEED WITH THIGHS OF STEEL

"Some of my best leading men have been horses."
ELIZABETH TAYLOR

Little girls dream of having a pony, though the closest most get is to harness a friend with skipping ropes and canter about the playground. Some girls never lose the yearning for a wild mount gripped between her thighs, a powerfully muscular form straining beneath her to be ridden into submission... before being rewarded with a brandy-soaked sugar cube.

Choosing Your Mount

Whether selecting a horse or a man, you need to check both beasts out for temperament to be as well matched as possible. If it's your first time, it's best to select a ride that will be gentler otherwise broken bones or a walk befitting John Wayne could put you off getting back in the saddle. If you are a more accomplished rider than a Jilly Cooper heroine, you should go for a more challenging mount.

Of course, without proper attention and vigorous exercise all creatures develop bad habits or 'stable vices'. Ensure your mounts don't become wayward by devising exciting exercises.

Attitude

Even if your mount is a whopper, never show fear. If you are good at masking your trepidation, he won't notice. A 'have a go' spirit is irresistible in an equestrian and a seductress.

TYPES OF STEED:

Shires suit ladies who like their mounts reassuringly deliberate and masculine, like an equine Sean Bean.

Arabians have lively dispositions and can take you on a thrilling ride, but they lack stamina. Thank God men are easier to train!

Dressage ponies are like girls – beautiful to behold, healthily competitive and with just enough wilfulness to make men take notice.

Colts are young, untamed and exhausting to break in which is perfect training for a wannabe cougar.

Shetlands are vicious bastards with short fuses and stature issues. These are traits best avoided in any species.

Reigning Supreme

Whips are useful if you want to control your mount's pace, but should never be used to excess. It is cruel to strike a horse, and over-use on a man could damage the diamanté handle and Argentine leather.

These stirrups are the only type a girl cherishes and are essential for raising her position, maintaining a lady-like gait and encouraging forward action.

A bit placed in the mouth helps a girl to control her mount expertly and steer him in the right direction, also useful if you want to shut up a lover.

Bareback riding is not for the faint of heart – best reserved for a mount you are in a long-term, trusting relationship with.

Distractions at the Stables

Sexy farriers are a rare breed and can do funny things to a girl with all that heat and molten iron being worked at in such a dominant manner. Stable hands are attractive to girls and why not? They love animals and don't mind doing dirty work.

WHAT TO WEAR

Hunting jackets are super sexy, especially if fitted. Red is preferred if you are all about the hunt and tweeds give a girl a classy appeal.

Jodhpurs are enchantingly snug and prove wonderfully frustrating for a lover to wrestle off.

Riding boots lend authority to a lady rider, and if you wish to make a man do something for you, make sure you wear them with nothing else.

The Dismount

Being graceful and gracious are paramount when dismounting. If you are coming down off a horse, you may find that some steps will help retain your dignity. If you are even extricating yourself from a lover the dismount is still important – steady yourself on him and make sure to say thank you.

'HERE COMES THE HOT STEPPER' —
THE WORLD IS YOUR CATWALK

Seductive possibilities can be had anywhere and the way a woman carries herself can have a striking effect on the men she passes by. If you lack belief in your walk, imagine yourself stalking the runway for a famed designer dressed in nothing but heels. Flashbulbs explode in unison with the crotches of rock stars in the front row – feel the difference in your gait and confidence? Pull it back a few notches and do it for real. You don't need to be a supermodel to move seductively. As Naomi Campbell demonstrates, it's not so much the strange model strut that demands adulation, but rather the attitude she poses when she walks.

The shorter a girl's stride, the more engaging it is to an alpha male. Tottering relays a message of submissive vulnerability, that you could easily be knocked to the ground and ravished. If you have the perfect geisha walk, be sure to match this with secret ninja skills to prove you are no push-over. Long strides tend to denote a leader rather than a follower, which is attractive to men who like their girls to be dominant and assertive.

Heels vs Flats

Heels obviously win for lengthening the leg and making a woman move in a more sensual manner, but they are agonising if worn for prolonged periods and terrible for covering any real distance. Flats can afford you an edgy sexiness, ankle boots are perfect, and, unlike a girl in heels, flat wearers will never exasperate their date by taking an age to walk five metres.

BRIEF ENCOUNTER — TRAIN ETIQUETTE

The sense of panic before the departure board announces a train, the paranoia of imagining someone fiddling with your luggage back in the racks while you are trapped in the centre of a carriage: all lend themselves beautifully to seduction if you are a masochist. But, if that impotent old rogue Hitchcock could turn trains into the setting for a steamy clinch, then you should have no problems.

HOW TO GET A SEAT

Play a game called 'How many gentlemen can I create?' This involves getting a man to give up his seat, even if you do not want it, by any means possible.

Perhaps unorthodox, but put your bag up your top and feign pregnancy. If this initially fails, freak him out by pretending your waters have broken (you'll need skilful timing and a leaking bottle of Evian). Voila, soon you will have your pick of any seat and he will always stand for pregnant women in the future.

Take crutches with you regardless of whether you need them. Men will be far more likely to stand for you if you are injured, rather than pregnant or old, as they can't ever imagine being the last two.

The most gratifying option is to look as inviting as possible. When confronted with a hot girl, most chaps want to at least give the impression of chivalry, though he may only offer you his knee – if he takes your fancy it'll beat standing.

Quiet Zones on trains are the perfect places for escaping inane monologues and engaging in quietly inventive games with a fellow commuter.

Let your body talk. Alluring journeys can start the minute you find an attractive man opposite you. Casually brush your neighbour's leg with your foot. If he reciprocates, place your foot a little higher. Before long he should be next to you, his coat over your lap and his hand furtively exploring your skirt. Catch his eye in the window as the world speeds by and you feel a rush of blood to the head. Silence is golden and unspoken encounters can be all the more precious.

Sleeper Trains

When it comes to rail travel this is by far the most attractive option, conjuring seductions of times gone by, of dusty lands, and heart-wrenching love affairs.

Unless you want to sleep with one eye open, it's wise to opt for a private cabin, then use your discretion as to who shares with you. There is a charm in going to bed with someone in one location and waking up with them somewhere completely different. Casual seductions are rarely so moving.

Lost Tickets

If you have multitudes of bags, it will be to your advantage – as I said before, men HATE ladies' bags and even an inspector won't want to be delayed by that sort of epic rummage-about. If that doesn't work, cry and explain you must have been pick-pocketed, even if memory tells you your purse is at home. Men hate tears more than bags, especially all-consuming sobs... he'll do anything to stop you crying, including letting you off a fine.

It is good to note that ticket inspectors are the only men on a train allowed to jolt strange females awake to scrutinise their credentials. Make sure no one encroaches on you in this manner unless invited.

Ah, the illusive and authoritative driver. Against all odds he aims to get you off on time, if only all men could be so diligent when it comes to a girl's needs.

Remember the emergency cord is not to be pulled just because you have not! If you have enjoyed the moment let your lover or the train rock you to a jubilant slumber.

GOING UNDERGROUND — SUBWAY ETIQUETTE

The Tube offers up a rich diversity of people and there is something about this subterranean world and all the choices it presents that means people do not behave in their right minds. The average commuter spends over a hundred entire days and nights on the Underground in their lifetime, so it would be a waste not to convert some of that drudgery into fun.

DOS AND DON'TS

Even if you are capable of carrying your heavy case, do pretend otherwise – it opens up an opportunity for someone to come to your aid.

Do not stand to the left of the escalators unless you are deliberately blocking the path of someone you want to know better.

Do offer your lap to a desirable commuter at peak times.

Do put money in a chap's hat and request he sings your favourite song. It will certainly get his attention, particularly if he isn't a busker.

Do carry a bottle of water with you, as it's not uncommon to get hot under the collar especially if you are the filling in a man sandwich. Douse yourself liberally.

Do help if a sexy chap faints – place a perfumed wrist under his nose and as he comes to, help rouse him with a restorative view of your cleavage.

Do read books with provocative titles (hint, hint) if you want to spell out your intentions to a fellow passenger. Be sure to look up, catch his eye and lick your finger before turning the page.

Do carry antibacterial wipes with you... even if a chap seems clean-cut you can never be too sure.

Do use the escalators as an excuse to give the eye to hot commuters.

Do take covert snaps of any chaps who take your fancy... it's not pervy if you have a blog.

Do pretend to pick something up off the floor as you pass the guy you fancy, say 'I think you dropped this' and hand him a note with your number on before alighting at your stop. Nothing chanced, nothing gained.

Do sit next to a guy you find attractive, open up your laptop and begin typing a Tube-based fantasy, pause and look away – people are nosey and he will read it. Then continue writing, adding a description of him. Again, pause and wait until you can feel him reading over your shoulder and then write 'So would you be interested in finding out how this ends?' Turn and gauge his response. He won't be terrified if you make your torrid tale fun.

Advantages of the Tube

The shuddering of a moving carriage lends a burlesque quality to a girl's breasts which attracts many fans of movement.

The overhead rails allow for subtle and massively charged hand flirting, so lightly slip your fingers over a stranger's – if his hand doesn't move away, you can increase the tension with a few soft and deliberate strokes.

Poles in a carriage are more affordable and easier to access than a gym, plus they allow the more confident and thrifty girl to have a workout while travelling. If you are not shy about your skills, do a few turns and slides to firm up your glutes and core, and earn extra cash between stops.

Be sure to familiarise yourself with all the lines, so you know which ones have the higher ratios of attractive men.

Follow a random stranger and see where it leads you, because it makes a nice change for a lady to be a sex pest.

Explore new areas, thinking of each journey as a mini holiday. Stick a pin in three parts of the subway map, then go forth and see what hidden beauty spots and eccentric characters you can find to fall in love with.

If it's a rainy day, why not hold an impromptu party on the Tube – invite friends and colonise a carriage. It's unusual, you can theoretically stay all day and each stop brings fresh blood.

Cramped conditions aren't all fun and games. If someone is trying to take unwanted liberties with you in such a situation, shout 'Please Mind My Gap, Swine'.

KM HIGH CLUB (MILES ARE FOR AMATEURS): JET SETTING

Selecting who you fly with is a bit like sizing up a boy, you want them to offer you an attractive package, be attentive to your needs and make sure you arrive thoroughly satisfied.

The airline you patronise often dictates your in-flight seduction options: if you like a bit of rough, go budget, but for pure sex appeal, there is nothing more attractive than reclining on a business-class Virgin.

Check-In

If there are delays, don't mope about, go exploring. With so many people in transit I am sure you can find someone to help you make time fly pleasingly.

Overweight luggage can be a costly error. Charm the pants (literally, if you are skilled) off the check-in attendant and if that fails tell them your bag has a thyroid problem.

Security

In these queues fear perfumes the air and even the most law-abiding citizen suddenly questions if they accidentally stuffed kilos of narcotics into one of their orifices. Remain calm and use it as time to scope out your fellow fliers.

If you have always longed for a sapphic experience, secrete jewellery into your gusset and enjoy as things get frisky with a security lady.

Never put anything in your hand luggage that you would be ashamed to have paraded in public – giant dildos and hand-cuffs can rouse curiosity from more than an X-ray monitor.

Duty-Free

Even if you are travelling for business, you should treat yourself. Have a few cognacs at the bar, purchase a camera, or lure a pilot off course – anything you need to do to ensure duty is forgotten and freedom is achieved. Remember to keep an eye on the time because gates will eventually close.

All Aboard

A window seat is perfect for a girl who enjoys breathtaking views of the world beneath her, especially if the view in the seat next to her leaves something to be desired. If you actually like the person/persons next to you, this gives you an excuse to brush past them if you need to stretch your legs.

Upgrading is notoriously difficult to achieve if you haven't made some sort of financial transaction. But don't be disheartened:

* If you are blessed with a chair that will not go into the upright position you could upgrade. This is where destructive DIY skills come in handy.

* Fainting or feigning illness is an effective way to bump yourself up, even if your only allergy is to cattle class.

* Go armed with a bottle of wine you know you are unable to travel with and offer it to the lady at the ticket desk. Upgrades have come from such acts, because there was no actual hint of a bribe and most people conceal an inner lush.

* If all this fails, insiders assure me that airline stewards sometimes respond positively to sexual favours.

Cabin crew are your main seduction rivals in the sky. They play to most men's fantasies by being attractive, in uniform and ready to tend to all their needs (and that is just the male stewards). If you want to out-do them, don a replica of the outfit worn by Angelina Jolie in *Sky Captain and the World of Tomorrow*. Men love a girl with an eye-patch.

Safety demonstrations are important and mildly amusing if you hum the Macarena very, very slowly in your head.

The more appreciative you are to the person tending to your needs, the more likely they will be to go all the way for you – and that applies to everything in life.

The most delightful moment a girl can have on a plane is when it trembles into life and you and your companion race to put your clothes back on and get into your seats before take-off.

Even if you are not in the least bit worried by turbulence, use it to your advantage. You can instantly establish more intimacy with someone you like the look of by grabbing their leg when you hit a stormy patch (though try to limit it to someone you are actually sitting next to).

HELLO BIG BUOY — YACHTING

Even if the closest you have ever gotten to a 60-footer is the lunchtime rush at Subway, there are still ways for you to cruise your way aboard a luxury vessel.

Hanging out in exorbitant Euro-trash marina bars that swim with vulgar oligarchs and an entourage with faces so stretched they could be hired out as trampolines is one option. They're perfect places to fish for invites but at what cost?

If you are landed by a seafaring playboy, don't be shocked if he requests you open up the poop deck when you come on board. Before you slap him it might be worth noting that it is actually part of the yacht.

If you'd rather hook up with a captain, remember it will take more than a trail of fish fingers and a net. Go on the Internet and find a captain you like the look of, before dropping him a line saying you are a naughty-call (phonetically it sounds plausible) journalist doing a piece on 'The World's Best Seamen' for an exclusive (and fictitious) publication. See if he bites.

If you must, use force to get what you want, but make sure you wear Vivienne Westwood for any acts of piracy. As you board a boy's vessel, let him know that you want neither his money nor his life, but rather a jolly (good) roger to help you develop your sea legs.

Listen: to 'Swept Away' by The XX to get you in a sexxy and sultry mood.

Watch: Dead Calm, because a lady should always know what to do if she is stranded at sea with Billy Zane and he becomes mad with want. It shouldn't be too problematic if you demonstrate you have (a) flare.

Don't Watch: Swept Away starring Madonna – it proved you don't have to be on a boat to feel seasick.

CHAPTER SIX

Something for the
weekend:
having fun

All work and no play would make life utterly grey, and sadly not in a *Fifty Shades* way, and thus weekends were invented to promote wild pursuits and charming bad behaviour. With so many possible activities to choose from, your downtime should never be dull.

DIRTY WEEKEND — FESTIVAL SURVIVAL

Your notion of a dirty weekend may involve a seedy motel room, a rotating waterbed, your face deep in a pillow and a man of ill repute wanting to plumb your hidden depths, but remember there are plenty more options to be had.

To connect with your basest self, you'd be wise to grab a guitar, some longhaired lovers and head to an outdoor music festival. With all that fresh air, sex, drugs and rock 'n' roll, you will be soon be immersed in utter filth…

Choosing a Festival

Love Box: One's a festival in a London park that is perfect if you don't like tents, as the only camping here comes courtesy of a majestic performance by Grace Jones. The other is a euphoric act involving a lady's most treasured part. After a day of dancing and social lubrication this is not beyond the realms of possibility.

Glastonbury: The ultimate festival, where the world's music giants provide the soundtrack as the masses get high on sex, music and debauchery… so much so that you NEED to roll around in the mud to get clean.

Sonar Barcelona: If you like your festivals like your men: Spanish, full of swagger and pumping hard, then this is the festival for you.

Port Eliot Literary Festival: Perfect for the girl who wants to improve her mind and partake in long, heated sessions with a bookish bit of crumpet.

Burning Man: If your idea of heaven is camping with a few thousand scantily dressed, beautiful radicals in the harsh Nevada desert, before setting fire to an effigy of a man, this is the festival for you. Burning Man prides itself on being a community-driven festival where events are dependent on participants creating shared environments of artworks, absurdity, and revelry. It is customary to gift other revellers with your own unique qualities and gifts – bear in mind it only lasts for a week.

Roskilde: A smorgasbord of world-class bands and hot Scandinavian men, and with over one hundred thousand attendees you should have no problem finding someone tasty. As if that weren't enough, they hold a Naked Run on the Saturday (hurrah for Denmark!) where women and men race to win the prize of a ticket to the following year's festival. Time to get in training or perhaps you prefer to spectate?

Benicassim: There could be worse ways for a girl to spend her time than heading to this festival in the stunning setting of Valencia. They play host to more rock-gods than you could shake a kilo of cocaine at, and there is a lot to be said for the swagger and sex appeal of the locals.

Primavera: If you like nothing better than unearthing new talent on and off the stage, this festival near Barcelona is where it's at. Big names also play but the real focus here is on independent music and bands that are fresh to the scene. So if you fancy bagging a musician before he gets global attention this is your ideal event.

Survival Tips

Before packing your camping bag with fashionable clothes, note that anything you wear is likely to end up at best soiled, and at worst becoming a biohazard. Choose clothes that you won't be sorry to say goodbye to, because you'll certainly be setting fire to more than a man's loins.

Festivals often take place in the summer – however, if you're in the UK it's likely it will be pissing down with rain. Still you could always ask a chap to rub some cream into a hard-to-reach place, and if you need cheering up why not suggest the G-spot?

You should always take a rescue remedy with you – not the sort that banishes flu, but a friend who can act as a wing woman helping you escape festival freaks.

A girl should always be prepared for a rainy day. Make sure you have plenty of condoms at the ready, as when the floodgates open you could get soaked.

Keep a stash of drinks in your quarters because even festivals have a cut-off point, the bars are expensive and the after-party is where you could experience the most intimate performances.

It's not a nuclear fallout so don't stockpile mountains of food because you'll have nowhere to store it all. Eggs, bacon, bread and a gas burner give a seductress the upper hand, particularly if conquests like their eggs fried and yours unfertilised.

Always stock up on things you suspect could run out quickly such as cigarettes, lip gloss, chewing-gum, baby wipes, knickers and most importantly… dignity.

Getting a good view of your much-loved act is no mean feat when you have to contend with a wall of people who aren't keen to offer up an easy passage, even if you promise that you will be gentle and smear them in Vaseline first. If you can't get to the front of the stage, try flirting with a statuesque man until he offers to put his head between your legs (no, not that – but maybe later) and raise you aloft so you don't miss anything.

Accommodation

Get a large tepee and scatter the floor with lots of soft cushions and rugs... Then fill liberally with sensual slaves for your own personal harem.

If glamping is more your style, why not do something unusual and hire an old gypsy caravan driven by a hot, bare-chested, bare-knuckled Romany and offer to read his tea leaves... the next morning.

A girl's beauty sleep can be adversely affected when camping, so either follow the crowd and renounce rest, or steal on to a handsome but chemically altered band member's tour bus and have a kip whilst he makes love to a sea of hallucinations.

Big festivals are ideal for multiple seductions and the sheer volume of people means endless scope for festival romances. If you want to embrace your saucy pagan festival goddess, find a pretty copse before laying yourself down in a circle of candles. Get a horny worshipper to incant praise to your natural beauty spots before offering him a sip from your furry cup.

Remember, if the yurt is rocking, he's either taken a ridiculous amount of Viagra or there has been a mass stampede – either way, you'll need to take refuge. What is the etiquette for getting your rocks off if you and a friend are sharing a tent? Even if you are off your tits (on the highs of life) you probably don't want to get intimate while your bezzie is lying beside you. If you both bring guys back simultaneously and can't decide who should get priority, just get the chaps to toss for it.

It is wise not to take a squeeze back to your pitch if you don't want to spend more time with a boy than you have to. Go to theirs instead because in a field hosting multitudes of revellers, it's unlikely they will be able to track you down again.

Going off on your own is important as it allows you to do as you please. It's wonderful for seeking out new tents, bands and men without having to factor in other people's whims. It is much easier to make exciting connections with people when solitary and increases the likelihood of an invite backstage.

Types of suitors you will find in various music tents:

R&B: Perfect if you want to be treated like a ho.

Rock: Perfect if you like sex and drugs.

Indie: Perfect if you like boys who do girls like their boys, who do boys like their girls.

Drum and Bass: Perfect if you like your organs to be rearranged with the twist of one knob.

Folk: Perfect if you like a man who is 70% beard, 30% cider.

Grime: Do I need to spell it out?

Country: Perfect if you like a man in heels with an achy, breaky part.

Nature Calls

Au Natural Pros: If it's good enough for bears...
Cons: 'If you go down to the woods tonight you'll be sure of a big surprise' (this could end up in the pro section).

Portaloo Pros: Some of them pipe muzak and what could facilitate a festively sluggish system more effectively than Genesis?
Cons: There's no such thing as a seductively surprised squatter, so get a friend to guard the door.

Backstage Convenience Pros: They are clean and roomy enough for a restoratively grubby encounter in the stalls, and the only Portaloos that guarantee a girl leaves on a high.
Cons: You could get trapped in one with Pete Doherty.

IBIZA UNCOVERED — BRIEFEST BREAKS

There has been a pervasive attitude since the 60s that anything goes on this island. Attracting partygoers, playboys and jet-setters, Ibiza is the spiritual home of the decadent and the diabolical. The fact it is such a free place allows it to be a true melting pot for all ages, sexual persuasions and beliefs. Here you can be anything you want, do anything you want, with anyone you want, take what you want, sleep when you want, dance how you want, listen to what you want – and that is truly appealing. Ibiza crackles with sexual charge and magnetic energy, enabling even the biggest wallflower to blossom into a Venus Guy Trap.

Do: Have it large! Unless you just don't think it is fitting for you.

Do: Enjoy the ecstasy a night of sexy tunes and rubbing against sweaty bodies on the dance floor engenders. Dancing is the perfect barometer for working out how good someone will be in bed, so be sure to display how rhythmic and flexible you are before engaging in further contact.

Do: Have a holiday romance even if it's with a long-term partner – the hedonism of the island will help you to recapture that initial spark.

Do: Dress provocatively, everyone else does, so you will feel more out of place if you play it safe. Complete your look with body paint, a liberal attitude and throng of buff gay men.

IN THE SADDLE — POLO MATCH

Polo: one a confection adored by the purple-rinse brigade and the other a sport beloved by (future) kings, the famous and posh totty with teeth that could give the ponies a run for their money.

Polo is a sport synonymous with luxury, where each horse is as expensive as a Lamborghini and the players have bluer blood than a high-quality vampire porno. This game is so elite even horses have a rider, which usually includes a bath filled with puppies and a vase of blue M&Ms.

A Cartier match is the perfect place to rub shoulders and potentially other parts with royalty, captains of industry, movie stars and, if you are feeling charitable, cast members from *Made in Chelsea*.

What You Need to Know

Play lasts ninety minutes and is divided into seven-minute play periods, proving short bursts of activity can be exciting. There are four players per team and the best-looking ones are the Argentinean side.

Remember to get into the spirit of things and show enthusiasm for the game as well as the men. Cheer on your favourite rider, otherwise he might not know how much you are enjoying yourself. At half time join the crowd in 'stomping the divots', which is the act of stamping clods of earth ripped up by play back into the pitch. Think Julia Roberts in *Pretty Woman*, though obviously without the financial transactions around seductions.

If you are having a picnic on the lawn and you would like someone to join you, approach him and innocently ask if he would like to have a 'roll' with you on your rug.

What to Wear

Think garden party chic with a simple vintage maxi dress and don't forget sunglasses to allow you to spy on people until you wish to be caught. For footwear, serious heels are only advisable if you wish to get stuck in the pitch and appeal to a man who can't resist coming to a girl's rescue.

If you are unsure about what scent to wear, why not spritz yourself in Big Pony, allegedly a perfume by Ralph Lauren.

When conversing with fellow spectators, do not recoil in horror or offer ointment to a chap who expresses a wish to show you his country pile. If you like a more arrogant gentleman play him at his own game and ask him if he would like to be your trophy lover. If you wish to turn down a boy's offer to get fresh at the match, be polite and present to him instead a mint with a hole.

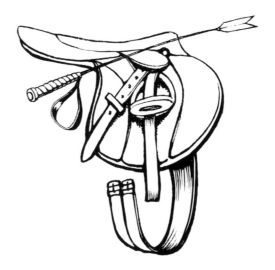

FAST MOVER — GRAND PRIX

Adrenalin-fuelled motor racing is undeniably exciting, and with all that testosterone speeding about it's a wonder ladies don't fall instantly pregnant the moment they enter the paddock.

If you think of motor racing only as a boring and loud spectacle for petrolheads, you need to take a moment to re-think. Shut your eyes and breathe in the deep smell of burning rubber and fuel, cloying in the hot air. Imagine vapour rising off the scorching track, and grease-covered mechanics sliding underneath you. Then comes the intoxicating roar of engines as they cut close to one another turning into the chicane. Metal ripping and flying through the air as two cars collide and a crowd of collective heartbeats hammer. Your victor takes to the podium as Champagne spray arcs over men in jumpsuits and soaks you, before your designated driver takes your tail for a spin. Better, right?

Wear something that errs on the side of smart and if you are hell-bent on wearing heels make sure you have a man to help prop you up, perhaps see if Bernie Eccleston is available.

Trackside

Earplugs are a must because these high-octane cars make a hell of a noise and plugs can be useful if you get stuck with the worst sort of motormouth.

Never stand by a crash barrier because a spare tyre flying toward a lady's face is rarely desirable in any circumstance.

Alternate drinking by availing yourself of other pleasures on offer in the paddock – you'll find manicurists, make-over artists, drivers talking about their careers. Some of these things will help relax you and one is sure to send you to sleep.

If you are not up to speed with Grand Prix drivers, you may not know who to support on the grid – here is a helpful guide for a girl who is more interested in men than cars:

Fernando Alonso who drives for Ferrari could be Javier Bardem if a girl viewed him tipsily from a distance.

Jenson Button is a blonde hottie who drives for McLaren, though be warned he's had more hot models than they've had hot meals.

Michael Schumacher is the star of the Mercedes team with looks suited to a mask and helmet, however there is something to be said for German precision.

Kimi Räikkönen drives for Lotus and is a fearless Nordic cutie – the perfect boy to support if you harbour pillaging fantasies.

Bruno Senna, nephew of the late pin-up and legend Ayrton, drives for Williams and proves that not all Brazilians are painful or leave you with a rash.

BEATING THE BUSH — COUNTRY PURSUITS

If the act of thwacking at undergrowth with a stick to unearth defenceless birds for hunters to shoot doesn't do it for you, perhaps suggest a less barbaric activity. Is that a shotgun in his trousers... God, I hope not for your sake!

Hunting is a controversial pastime – even more so if fervently pursuing a spirited two-legged creature cross-country. A girl would never be so crude as to hunt down an utterly defenceless man, because where would the fun be in that? Opt for a ladylike ride upon a two-pommel saddle to give you extra security as you jump into action.

When armed with something loaded and dangerous remember to aim with care, whether it's a gun or a proposition, to make sure you hit your target. Test out which of your eyes is dominant, this will be the one you train on your mark, and as is customary in shooting and seduction, don't let him out of your sights until you have hit him with your best shot. Don't get trigger-happy – all too easily guns can prove how dangerous a simple squeeze of the finger can be.

When shooting, a girl should consider bore size – not the measurements of a dull companion, rather the kick and power of your gun. Like a tedious fellow though, the greater the bore the more painful a girl will find the experience, but it's rare that an encounter with a ghastly man results in a girl's shoulder turning black and blue after his butt has rammed it. A heavy 12-gauge shotgun is more suited to a shooter with experience, or a lady who can deal with big impacts, but if you like to be treated gently then a 16-gauge shotgun would be appropriate.

Once the gun is loaded, keep it broken open over your arm until it is your turn. Firing prematurely is a costly mistake and can surprisingly also affect girls. Stand at an angle of about 40 degrees to the left or right of your target and lift the gun so the shotgun's butt (the wooden end) is resting snugly against your shoulder to reduce kickback when you fire. It should be positioned so that your cheek caresses the wood and you can align your sight along the barrel. Switch off the safety catch as your male companions watch you with fierce admiration, and then breathe, aim, fire.

Never point a loaded gun at anyone, even if you are having murderous thoughts and you think you could get away with it. If you don't like guns, but like the idea of a half-cocked double-barrel on your arm, offer to escort a posh boy on a shoot.

Constitutional Rights

If you really want to feel the restorative benefits of nature, there is nothing like a hike. Sun, rugged terrain, staggering views and exercise can only be improved upon if one goes adventuring in the buff with a companion or group (depending on your preferences of course). All that fresh air, bracken and the sting of nettles smarting over the calves or buttocks does wonders for a girl's circulation, constitution and earthy sexual pull.

Tempting Fête

Quaint village communities often come together to eat cake and gossip about the bored rural seductress. It's frightfully easy to cause a scandal provided you are happy to be on everyone's lips. This can be achieved by:

✳ Enjoying a good tug of war with the boys.

✳ Not being shy about your lovely bunch of coconuts.

✳ Possessing an awesome aptitude for the cheese-rolling competition (a girl who goes to such lengths to get her hands on an Edam is a rare and prized thing amongst men).

LADIES' DAY — A DAY AT THE RACES

This event is less about horses and more about being the most stylish girl in the paddock, but don't fall into the trap of sporting a hat that could be mistaken for a UFO. It might attract photographers but not men. It is notoriously difficult to kiss while wearing a wide-brimmed hat, but it can help intensify cravings – try to tilt your head to an agreeable angle to plant a smacker without removing someone's eye. Alternatively choose something elegantly eye-catching and more passion-friendly.

Betting

When it comes to horses, quit while you are ahead, and when it comes to men, quit if they refuse you head.

If you've backed a loser, you should accept your loss with equanimity or try and sell him to the knacker's yard. However they may refuse on the grounds that he's a man.

Don't gloat. If you've gotten lucky once or multiple times and are seriously flush(ed), enjoy the moment quietly – you don't want everyone going after your ride.

Keep excited screaming to the minimum because both seduction and being a gracious winner call for a little decorum, especially when in public.

The Knowledge

Putting money on the nose only ever gives you a return if your boy finishes first – girls would make a killing if they could make this bet about their lovers.

Avoid real outsiders even if they seem like an attractive challenge – there's a reason why no one fancies them.

If you can't afford to lose, don't risk the gamble; which is equally true of seduction and horses.

POP-UP, EXCLUSIVE AND LIMITED EVENTS

Every week there's a new dining trend or faddy drinking den opening, attracting hordes of curious people, and if an event has more buzz around it than a rampant rabbit you should definitely give it a go.

Secret Cinema is the perfect date venue for a discreet tryst between a girl and amative film buff. These events often have dress codes, which can add to your fun if you wish to role play for extra warmth under a blanket in the back row.

Speakeasies are all the rage – here drinks are served in teapots and filled to the brim with something as strong as Rohypnol. Bear in mind that if you need to drug him to bed him, you are certainly selling yourself short.

ROCK HARD — CLIMBING

Climbing is the sexiest thing you can do in a harness with most of your clothes on. Those attracted to climbing are generally enthusiasts of extreme physical challenges and magnificent natural beauty. Others go because they like muscular backs, peachy bums and want to be challenged by someone's physicality. A girl who climbs benefits from toned muscles she never even knew she had, and sexy instructors who are always on hand to help a lady reach new highs.

When climbing or seducing, be aware that patience can be a virtue, and if you are close to reaching the peak bear in mind it can take others longer.

Leaving your area cleaner than when you found it, by picking up any debris related to your activities and wiping any surfaces or clothing to remove anything slippery, is just good manners.

Keeping the noise down shows you can be sensitive to the solitude enjoyed by other people around you... put a hand over his mouth if need be.

IMPRESS A BOY WITH YOUR CLIMBING KNOWLEDGE WITH THE HELP OF THIS GLOSSARY:

'Dirt-Me' needs to be shouted when you want to be lowered to the ground, it's up to you if you want him to follow.

'Elvis leg' is an excessive shaking of the leg due to exhaustive activity, made more attractive if he can do a tuneful rendition of 'Love Me Tender'.

A 'Flash' is a first attempt at a climb with no falls, rather than a cry given when a climber spots an exhibitionist.

'Jamming' refers to wedging one's fingers, hands and feet in responsive cracks – surprisingly hard in both climbing and the seduction of men.

'Monkey-toe' is thankfully not a new peril of clinging clothes, but a foothold that proves a girl is queen of the swingers.

A 'Shock-load' can refer to the result of a surprise climbing manoeuvre or an unfortunate tryst.

'Smearing' is mercifully all about fancy footwork and has nothing to do with gynaecologists.

CORE VALUES — RULES OF THE GYM

The gym is fertile ground for seducing fit men. You can casually browse before deciding if you would like to enlist a chap in a one-on-one workout. It won't shock you to learn that men go to gyms primarily to check out women, and girls go to gyms to exercise and check men out (even at the gym girls can multitask).

A girl working out is a huge turn-on to men, in and out of the gym. Boys are especially fond of the sight of a girl on a thigh adductor (lifting a weight by spreading her legs apart or squeezing them together), or bent compromisingly over a Swiss ball. Perhaps this is why these two pieces of equipment are rarely ever free.

If women didn't go to the gym, men would just go on beer and curry binges, so by turning up girls provide men with a motivational service that not only improves their life expectancy, but also gives them someone they want to work toward.

The hormonal effects of a workout are seriously beneficial to increasing your sex appeal. A good session increases the testosterone levels in men and makes them feel hornier, and the endorphin release a girl experiences has a similar impact.

Locker rooms are increasingly like Eastern European holiday camps, leaving precious little to the imagination. Try not to be prudes, girls – go native and shake what your mama gave you. After all, isn't the point of going to the gym about building body confidence?

Even if your gym is filled with eye-candy, there will still be certain specimens who are best avoided:

✳ Take, for example, a chap whose arms are so big he could be confused for triplets, calls guys 'girlfriend' and spends an inordinate amount of time in the sauna. He might be just your type but sadly, and don't take this personally, you won't ever be his.

✳ Any man who is having a serious love affair with his own reflection should be avoided at all costs because he only has eyes for one person, himself.

✳ Marvel at the missing link who grunts like he is birthing the biggest baby ever delivered. He will be easy to spot because he is curiously unblessed by a neck, and when he walks sparks fly due to the friction created when his massive thighs rub together.

If you spot a boy procrastinating by a piece of equipment or the water fountain, this is a perfect opportunity to approach him – he is not engaged in any activity and doesn't appear to be in a hurry to get back to his workout. When a guy keeps looking at you, especially if you catch him checking you out, this is the best indicator of how receptive he is to your fitness and he is definitely an admirer.

A good bra in the gym is like a good man in your life, both should completely support you no matter what you do.

Spinning is one of the most hardcore workouts and it can provide you with a choice of motivational things to focus on, such as hitting your fitness goals, improving your breathing rate or meditating on the tight bum of the cute boy in front.

If you crave that extra push when exercising, nothing beats a man who knows how to help you reach your physical peak. One type of personal trainer will make you do things you never thought were physically possible... the other type will just shout at you and make you do squat-thrusts in a rainy park until you cry.

When it comes to the gym, it's 'no pain, no gain', so try to focus less on the expense and arduousness of membership and seek to exploit as many of the exciting benefits as possible.

CHAPTER SEVEN

These wwwebs we weave: a guide to technology

Just when you think mobiles and laptops can offer a girl everything she wants, consider that they've yet to make apps which give you an orgasm, cuddle you, or throw their old pants on the floor to give you something to rail against.

If it gets to the stage when you spend so much time online or on the phone that you get withdrawal shakes when you log off, it's time to don a hot frock, slip into some heels, go out and get your life back.

> *"Ayo, I'm tired of using technology,*
> *why don't you come sit down on top of me?"*
> 50 CENT

YOU'VE GOT MALE — THE ETIQUETTE OF ONLINE CORRESPONDENCE

Social media, Internet networking and online dating have made it possible for even the busiest woman to enjoy time-efficient forays in seduction.

Creating an excellent email or message that will grab the attention of that certain someone comes down to three things:

✳ Firstly, the subject should be short, concise and enticing enough to pique a boy's curiosity.

✳ Secondly, consider the body of your message which should be as tempting as your own and contain questions or matters that inspire a responsive interplay and where possible threaten to corrupt his internal hard-drive.

✳ Lastly and crucially comes the sign-off – you must never end with 'Best' because this is the seductive equivalent of saying 'you are like a brother to me'. If you don't know him that well, refrain from putting 'Love', and never use an emoticon to convey your lust because that is the virtual equivalent of tugging a guy off with a hand puppet.

Tailor your letters according to the recipient. If he is an intellectual be thought-provoking, and if his brain is firmly in his pants be more descriptive and playful. Play to your strengths and if you are not a great writer you could always use visuals, but don't send anything that you would be ashamed to see in the national press. Increase the suggestiveness of your emails gradually – too full-on too soon and he will quickly go offline.

Always check the address before you press send because sending mail about someone to them by accident is an awful giveaway, especially if you want to play things cool. Worse still is sending something saucy to an inappropriate candidate by mistake – it could result in a family member needing therapy and awkward silences at Christmas.

Marking someone down for excessive exclamation mark usage, unless you concur with the urgency of his or her sentiments, is harsh but acceptable. Ditto the use of nauseating abbreviations such as 'I fink U n Me Shld Fuk 2night'. There is no excuse for scrimping when it comes to desirous exchanges.

Never reply too rapidly, nor leave a response too long, and if a chap doesn't reply to a highly confidential document within 48 hours it's time to shut him down.

Remember that any information you send to a suitor once sent cannot be retrieved. You must be completely happy to take ownership of anything you put out there, because once it's bouncing around in cyberspace it's there for good. Text, images and recordings can be used by anyone of a less reputable nature in order to exploit, upset or intimidate you... so if you want some bartering power, make sure you have a backup file of incriminating evidence about them.

BOOTY CALL — TELEPHONIC ALLURE

An excellent manner and a sultry phone voice are imperative when you want to fully engage someone in an intriguingly sensuous exchange. It's the most enjoyable way to utilise your monthly minutes.

Telephone Voice

Every girl has one and can modify hers depending on who she is talking to. The tone you employ when talking to your bank manager or your lover, though subtly different, will have the same intent – wanting a suitable return from anything you invest in them.

Always be clear about your desires because mumbling what you want to do to someone will cause your message to lose its potency if they have to keep saying 'that sounds good, what was the last bit though?' Soft, playful and a little breathy or husky may be clichéd but it's a sound starting point. Too breathy or husky will not so much say sexy as consumptive.

NEVER use a baby voice – if you both like it, you might want to ask yourself if there is something deeply questionable about him and regressive about you.

Always smile when conversing on the phone as it lends a richness and inviting quality to your voice and suggestions.

Dial-a-Date

It is wonderful to be spontaneous, but if you are in the mood for a call of the wild, it is wise to check your playmate isn't otherwise engaged. If they are at work or in a tricky environment your suggestive offerings could be met with monosyllabic answers, which will prove frustrating for both of you.

It can feel a little alien or silly the first time you attempt phone sex, but try to relax as best you can and let your mind get busy with scenarios you can bring to life with genuine gusto. The more you practise, the more you will recognise when it would be beneficial to your exchange and enjoyment to be authoritative and when to be compliant.

Adopting a conspiratorial and naughty tone is perfect for helping to reveal and tease out secret desires and using pauses allows your phone buddy to take the lead.

SET THE SCENE

Build up a depiction of where you are and what you are doing until he yearns to infiltrate that vision with dastardly desires of his own. You can either go all the way to climax with him or drive him wild and pretend you got cut off.

'It's so warm, I have to take some clothes off' is a good starting point. Talk him through this act and even if you are wearing sweat pants or think you look like crap, it doesn't matter because he can't see you. Paint the picture of yourself you most want him to see. All he will be able to think about is you disrobing.

'It's so good to hear your voice, I was just lying in bed thinking about you.' Simple, effective and guaranteed to make him ache for more graphic information.

Give him praise with appreciative moans when he is doing a good job of storytelling and redirect him when you feel he is getting in a tangle – satisfaction is key.

If a boy rings and asks seductively 'what are you doing?', never reply with something like 'cleaning the bin' unless you can turn it into the sort of grubby account you'd both benefit from.

If your playmate has a similar name to another person in your phone, be sure to make suitable distinctions in their entries, e.g. 'Big John' and 'Uncle John', otherwise you could end up with severely crossed wires.

Keep a note of the times a suitor tends to call because if it's always after 11 p.m., you know he will only ever be your buddy with a capital F.

POKE(H)ER — RULES OF SOCIAL NETWORKING

Attention spans wane in these domains due to an overload of stimuli, so girls, to attract a boy's full attention you need to find an economical and arresting way to make them stop and take notice of you.

Boys and girls are equally guilty of stalking each other on social networking sites, so it is not a bad idea to upload well-selected profile pictures. Excessive self-portraits complete with porn-pouts make a lady look narcissistic and cheap and can turn a boy off.

Highly compromising photos will only serve to put off potential suitors and employers and leave your inbox filled by dubious, illiterate men. Don't forget they can be easily down-loaded by men (including ones you don't know) just so they have some wank material. Bukhaki is not the aim of this game. Showing a little skin tastefully is much more alluring, perhaps a flash of shoulder or back which will give you the erotic lure of a naughty Victorian.

Information

Every social networking site has a section that acts like a web version of Cilla Black: 'What's your name, where d'ya come from and when did you last get poked?' They can prove invaluable sources for 'researching' (stalking is such an ugly word) a chap you fancy or attracting him to your profile.

Be as honest as you can with your profile while retaining a certain allure and don't create an online persona you can't live up to, no matter how tempting. It's easier to give the best version of ourselves through the mask of the Internet – these personas are not fake, just not quite the whole truth.

Knowledge is power and the information you can extract from a profile allows you to gauge how compatible you are and will help you write funny and engaging posts on his wall and send cheekier messages to his inbox.

Remember that the more beautiful and pure something is, the easier it will be to corrupt online. Start searching out men you'd like to ruin.

Beware the curse of putting your relationship status on display. It's like getting a boy's name tattooed on you – it's less painful, but both are the kiss of death.

Always set your chat profile to hidden so that you can see if a guy you like is online without him thinking you spend every waking moment lurking about.

Try to give a new suitor the benefit of the doubt if he comes across as charmless and unattractive on screen, when in real life he might be happily the reverse – not everything translates well online.

Flirting in this way can build up impossible standards on both sides that can only be altered with real interaction... so girls, don't forget to go and get sexy in the real world.

TEX-TUAL — RULING BY THUMB

Texting to attract someone's attention is a nuanced activity and demands careful thought, because a single well-crafted text could help you both to stimulate and press each other's buttons.

There is nothing remotely seductive about abbreviations and a text saying 'I'd Luv 2 C U cum' would only be sexy to R2D2. Use proper sentences to attract desirable adult ripostes.

When trying to be mysterious and cool, remember that excessive capital usage is as advantageous to textual seduction as a bullhorn is to Chinese whispers.

Correct punctuation is imperative if you don't want to send the wrong message, for example a text saying 'I love cooking my family and my dog' would have benefited enormously from a little more attention.

Even if you are impatient by nature, responding to each text the moment they arrive doesn't allow for any tension – be measured.

If you are in a social situation with your partner and it is not appropriate to tell him you are feeling randy, texting becomes a useful tool.

A girl who is glued to her phone on a date will find it only translates as 'I'm really into you' if she is a mute and that is her only way to communicate with her companion.

SEX TEXTING

'I keep thinking of what happened last night. Fancy a repeat performance?' is a great way to affirm that you enjoy his company. Even if his schedule is busy, it will make him want to have a cheeky shift about.

'I can't decide which lingerie to wear tonight... if only I had a second opinion.' If he doesn't get back to you immediately, it's probably because his smartphone just fainted.

FRENCH LETTER — PUTTING PEN TO PAPER IN ANY LANGUAGE

As Muhammad Ali once said 'There are two powers in this world, the pen and the sword. There is a third power stronger than both, women.' With this in mind, consider that meaning is derived not only from what a girl says but how she chooses to say it, and in a world where cold screens attract prose devoid of character expressive hand-penned letters become the tonic.

Handy-Work

The letter gives the kiss a run for its money when it comes to romantic, communicated art-forms, and it is undeniably evocative and sensual to arrive home to find a beautiful envelope that is satisfyingly thick, with exquisite handwriting, waiting for you.

Heartfelt writing and the time spent drafting a letter effects your recipient on a deep level, allowing him time for a greater appreciation of what is written and the attentiveness you have displayed. They convey more to the recipient than a quickly knocked-out email, with the fountain pen licking at a page as though it were a lustful tongue leaving an imprint of your thoughts.

Seductive letters can be stored for the sensually leaner years – their tactile quality, the hint of perfume upon them and charged declarations can rekindle long-forgotten sensations of desire. They are the treasured gifts and possessions of those who favour old-school seduction over instant gratification.

A girl needn't be a mistress of calligraphy to make an impact on a boy she is writing to. It's best to be simple and chic in style, avoiding any sort of sweeping gesture. If your handwriting leaves little to be desired, use an old-fashioned typewriter and channel provocative writers of times gone by, perhaps Anaïs Nin. There is a pleasingly fetishistic quality to striking the barely yielding keys and marking your paper with letters like a form of branding.

Don't forget that a handwritten letter is not only a rare thing of beauty, it is also a bold statement. When you send one, you are asking for someone's time and consideration, and offering the challenge of an accordant response. These correspondences take effort, they give away a lot about the writer, and they show that you are a deliberate seductress, not some wham-bam, thank-you-man type. It shows style, class and your ability to take your time when getting your message across.

If you must, draft the letter as explicitly as you like and then write it once again in a more subtle, veiled form... just raise the veil enough so he can glimpse something that will make him hunger for more correspondence. The better the quality and more expensive the paper you use for your final draft, the more intoxicating your sentiments will be.

Most importantly, when writing a letter a girl must create it with only the recipient's eyes in mind as it will make your expression more direct and evocative, rather than self-conscious. A loved letter can be kept in a jacket pocket and re-read over and over, until it has become tattered by adoration and disbelief that something so precious could come into a boy's possession.

UP CLOSE AND PERSONAL —
WEBCAMS AND IM

Instant Messaging

If you initiate the messaging, then it is your responsibility to be engaging and interesting to pull them in. Because these conversations can be speedy, you might need to practise typing one-handed.

A boy you are messaging could be at work or in a situation that will not facilitate well-timed or in-depth responses – a girl could find that just as she reveals exactly what she wishes her boy were doing to her under his desk, he unceremoniously disappears from the chat. Not great for a girl's ego, but remember that he may not have the freedom you have in his given environment.

Webcams

These are perfect if you and a lover are conducting a long-distance affair, because even though you may be in different time zones, why should your erogenous zones suffer? It is a great aid in reducing the temptation of straying from a partner if you are separated for a period of time.

Make sure the lighting is right: lit from underneath most things look demonic – instead stick to soft, flattering and overhead. Try and test different lighting as you stand close to a mirror. When you are happy, you are ready for lights, webcam, and action.

If you live in a shared house and don't want to limit yourself to the bedroom, make sure your housemates are out and your front door is double-locked. They may wonder why but it beats them finding you in a compromising situation on the kitchen table with your laptop between your legs.

Never start a webcam message nude, you need to take your time and there is always the chance that the person you are expecting will not be the first person you see.

Get your boy to describe a fantasy involving you, talk it through like foreplay, before you get him to direct you – don't be afraid to improvise when you think a scene could be improved upon.

GIRLS ON FILM — HOME-MOVIES

Making a sexy home-movie demands a well-crafted story, plenty of action and a thoroughly trusted co-star who is generous about sharing the love and the limelight with a girl.

If you want to see how not to make a dirty movie, have a look at Paris Hilton's charming rom-com. If texting during intercourse, displaying zero chemistry, and ghastly night vision do it for you, perhaps rethink your movie career.

For any performance, practice makes perfect, so if a boy is trying to negotiate a movie deal with you, say it is on the strict proviso of plenty of rehearsals and a screen test. If you absolutely hate the finished article at least you can say you tried, but insist on the tape being either destroyed or leaked especially if you're a struggling singer, actress or heiress.

Any good actress knows that a contract is vital when a girl wants to ensure she will not be exploited – when it comes to intimate affairs this is doubly important. Never, ever do anything on film that you wouldn't allow off-screen. Know your boundaries. Some things are not supposed to be trapped on celluloid... they are for memory alone.

CHAPTER EIGHT

Working girl: office relations

Not every girl has a job she feels passionate about and, like finding a satisfying lover, it can take years of laborious searches and numerous positions before you find the thing that brings out the best in you. A diligent girl can uncover a wealth of excitingly seductive prospects between the water cooler and the helpdesk.

SNAKES AND LADDERS — GETTING AHEAD (WITHOUT SNAGGING YOUR STOCKINGS)

A girl must demonstrate passion and drive to arouse excitement in her colleagues and clients, as well as talent and ability. When developing client rapport, make sure you bend backwards to help relations evolve – you'll find regular Pilates and a decent chiropractor are invaluable.

Demonstrate adaptability in the work place. Are you freaked by management restructures? What about late nights? What if your boss rams more at you? Will you offer him an unobstructed passage?

If your boss complains that everything feels stagnant, offer some fresh business proposals. If he propositions you in an untoward fashion, tell him to try and patch things up with his wife.

Being a visionary in the workplace means you need to have your eye on multiple balls to ensure you are on top of your game. Second-guess powerful allies' desires and always be ready to deliver your goods before they figure out that you are exactly the sort of girl they were looking for.

Ask yourself where you want to be and what sort of position you really hunger for. Are you a girl who envisages herself sat in the boss's chair, Manolos on the desk as you call the shots? What will you sacrifice to get there? Your social life, your morals, a goat? You should never compromise a goat.

If you want to be elevated through the ranks, you should scope out who you're up against. Woo your work rivals because a working girl should 'keep her colleagues close, but keep a closer eye on stiff competition'.

Rising Through the Ranks

At work socials people usually drop their guard, which offers advantages a girl should take. Sharing things shows trust or that you have plied a colleague with multiple Cock Sucking Cowboys.

Play the game by doing things like laughing at your boss's jokes or pretending he is good at his job – it's sort of like a sympathy shag, but without the desire to scrub yourself clean afterwards.

No matter how demeaning or ghastly a task may seem, do it with cheer and enthusiasm, though not too much enthusiasm as your boss may think you have a penchant for grubby work. If you can be adaptable you will be seen as invaluable.

Annual Review

A girl should always prepare for this meeting by creating a file she updates periodically with her accomplishments, including appreciative letters from clients praising your abilities, though only include ones related to work admiration.

Outline the contributions you have made that have increased revenue for the company, like winning over a hard-to-get client – perhaps leave out the part about more than company shares going up.

It pays to be familiar with the assessment process, and if you are doing a self-review get a copy as early as possible to allow you more time to craft your responses. 'I am the best thing that ever happened to this company, show me the money' may be the truest statement ever writ, but unfortunately not everyone can handle the truth.

Remember that salary increases are for work that exceeds the demands of your ordinary job description, so make sure the lengths you go to are within the law and repeatable.

A girl should always have a list of goals and be able to tantalisingly demonstrate to your boss that when it comes to scoring you are in the premier league. Always be prepared to give feedback as your boss may put you on the spot. Be as truthful as you can be and instead of venting at him, give some constructive problem-solving ideas:

Boss: '—— what do you think of my six-pack?'

You: 'Mr ——I think that a pay rise would go a long way in making me reconsider reporting your inappropriate behaviour.'

A girl's survival of a review demands that she is prepared for both the positive and the negative, and no matter how good she is, even in seduction, there is always room for improvement.

It never hurts to let your boss or lover know you are in demand – both will clamour to win you back if you let them think you will go with a rival.

Being a team player can enable you to build workforce morale, but save proper bonding exercises for someone special.

Multitasking: Appearing Busy Despite Doing Precious Little

Without access to the Internet and its manifest temptations, how could the female workforce justify spending so long glued to a screen? It's not as if girls' browsing histories lead to devastating viruses all over a company system – they leave hardcore offending for tangible moments, not virtual ones.

Procrastination is one of the most seductive pursuits known to the working girl because you know you should really be focused on that crucial marketing campaign, but the forbidden keeps on calling you: 'Just one more jaunt on Asos! Just one more trip to Ratehisface.com!' Procrastinators may happily spend the whole day in bed, but at least there they'd be more inclined to make the most out of their business.

It is vital a girl breaks up her working day with daydreams or flirting, these little thrills will stop her from getting burnt out because all work and no play is enough to drive any lady bonkers.

If your boss thinks a job should take you 50 minutes and it only takes you 20, why not use the remaining time for your own interests? He won't find out as long as you look as busy as a beaver.

And it's important for the working girl to note that being anally clean is only desirable if you are interested in bum deals. When it comes to the office, business debris must be artfully strewn on your desk to make it look as though you are slogging your arse off.

Keep work applications open on your screen ready to mask any forbidden sites you are illicitly viewing, and if you are on instant messenger promoting yourself to a professional suitor avoid typing furiously, no matter how urgent. Business typing is punctuated by moments of reflection and revision, so make your detours seem as genuine in pace as possible.

Cosy up to the IT department and get them to override any Big Brother monitoring your company may have enforced, because screwing the system is tremendously satisfying.

If you need something a bit more exciting to perk up your day, book a fake meeting with a colleague who is keen to prove himself to you. If questioned about this unscheduled meeting, say you were discussing the possibility of a 'merger between our two working bodies'. Alternatively get a sexy wordsmith to send you important-looking documents by sign-for courier with 'Classified: For urgent attention of' written on it. You may need to book a meeting room again for some quiet time. If called on, your whereabouts have an almost true, work-related back-up story: 'I was going over a client's growth projection'.

Freelance procrastination takes things to another level and a girl could literally do anything to stave off actually working. However, you also have a boss you love and respect so perhaps you'll actually get more done.

Because You're Worth... More – Getting That Pay Rise

Money and power are synonymous in the workplace, and though a girl's morals have rarely ever been increased by a pay rise, her bargaining power certainly improves. Knowing your own value is important and anything less won't do, and although a gentle slap in your face may work during a sexy tryst, I never heard of an enjoyable one from a pay review.

A girl should prove why she's an asset to her department, perhaps by applying her unique personal touch when dealing with a tricky client outside of office hours, especially if the client can't get enough of her hands-on approach. When the client sings your praises, your boss should see you get the remuneration you deserve. By developing new skills, you become more valuable to your company, and training can be just as advantageous if you want to reprogramme a boss or lover.

KNOW HOW TO NEGOTIATE WITH A TRICKY BOSS

If male:

You could be the hardest working team member easily exceeding all your targets and still be overlooked. If this is the case, you can either:

    a) Show him you have balls (any literal interpretation of this will backfire horribly) and challenge him as to why you haven't been promoted.

    b) Kiss his arse – before you pucker up, really assess how much shit you can take.

    c) Blackmail is an ugly word – use 'employment progression through incriminating visual/audio aids' instead.

If female:

    a) Flatter her by saying 'I appreciate your strength' – this may help the witch mellow and allow her to see a potential ally in you. She needn't know that by strong you meant 'grimly impenetrable'.

b) Seduce and confuse her inner lesbian with innuendo-laden business jargon – 'I want to get in bed with you on this matter' – and actively demonstrate you are keen to move your relationship forward.

c) If you work for yourself, why not award yourself a glowing self-appraisal before giving yourself the utterly justified title of 'Queen of fucking everything'. You can celebrate with a kneeling squire.

Fire Hazard – How to Sack Someone

Sackings are not unlike saying goodbye to a lover – they're unpleasant and emotional, though break-ups rarely come with the added benefit of security to help remove those who are radically in denial.

Avoid doing a Donald Trump – for a start, toupees look ghastly on girls, and barking 'You're Fired' lacks panache. Let a boy down as gently as you can, especially if you think he could be of use to someone else: 'Look, it didn't work out here, but maybe I could have a word with some contacts and see if they have a suitable opening you could fill.'

It is never easy letting someone go, especially if you like a guy, so if your hands are tied… perhaps wait until you are in a less vulnerable position before breaking the bad news.

It's important that when you let a guy go, you allow him some dignity and the words you choose are really important. If you're about to hurt someone, try to go easy because excess salt makes Margaritas taste foul and wounds smart like crazy. 'It's not me, it's you' works just as badly in the workplace.

If he asks questions like 'Is anyone else involved?' be gentle with him. A man's ego is fragile – don't let him know you replaced him with a surprisingly basic robot (though the attachments alone can do things he'd need serious retraining to achieve).

Warnings usually precede sackings and break-ups, so it is wise to give someone a fair chance to up their performance, but in both cases, if this isn't properly heeded, it's game over.

If you want to get to the root of an unproductive boy's issue, get him on his own and explain that you have serious concerns about his overall performance, but want to help him to overcome whatever is holding him back. A girl who shows a real concern for those under her has all the hallmarks of a great manager and considerate lover.

If you find yourself facing possible dismissal, see if you can convince your boss to give you a second chance. If your boss gives you an unpleasant ultimatum such as 'Fuck me or you're fired', tell him where he can stick it before you thoroughly shaft him... at a tribunal.

HOW TO CONDUCT AN OFFICE AFFAIR

Nearly 60% of office workers have at some point sealed the deal with a workmate, with a lesser number going on to date or marry that distracting someone. Look around the office. It may be time to be more ambitious.

Offices are microcosms of activity where business and pleasure oft collide, and some girls can be more 'accident'-prone than others. If you embark on an office fling and it goes wrong, you can't easily escape each other and that can make for awkward working dynamics. Ask yourself if a fumble in the stationery cupboard is worth potentially losing your job over.

Offices are epicentres of gossip, and the cloak-and-dagger courtiers of Elizabeth I would be hard pressed to keep up with the level of rumour spreading in an average office. Remember that the working 'dating pool' is potentially limited, especially if you are in a small company, and that can create a rather incestuous, not to mention bitchy, environment. Should you choose to embark on a work affair with a boy, you need to be ultra-discreet and select your partner in misdemeanours wisely.

If your company has a strict 'no dating' policy, you might want to check with HR that you haven't started working at Hooters by mistake.

Do you like your job more than a boy? Does he like you more than the job? Perfect, he can leave if things go wrong. Don't lose a job you love just because a boy turned your head.

GOOD SERVICING — HOW TO PLEASE TRICKY CLIENTS

Tricky clients are like the nightmare lover you can't escape – narcissistic, needy and wholly unaware of how much you do for them. When a client continually places unreasonable expectations upon a girl, she must try to negotiate a mutually beneficial arrangement to see that neither party feels compromised.

Clients who are indecisive are the curse of the working world and a girl must either exercise extreme patience or find a way to seduce them round to her way of thinking.

If you have worked yourself to the bone for a client or paramour who is unappreciative, you can resolve NEVER to engage with them again. Warn other interested parties to steer clear, because in sex and business reputation precedes a man.

Some tricky clients have their benefits – all the stress they provide is great for instant weight loss and seductresses love a good challenge.

With any dwindling or bombastic relationship, if you can still see a glimmer of the beautiful thing that made you want to team up with someone in the first place, you need to be sure they also think it's worth fighting for. For the best results, lavish the other person with attention and rekindle their passion to remind them of how much potential your union still has. Even if a client/man drives you mad, they may be too good to lose.

CHAPTER NINE

Home is where the harlot is: delicious domesticity

What is a domestic goddess? Like Aphrodite (the Greek goddess of pleasure) sat in her shrine/house as the faithful come to worship at her door with offerings of delectable devotion. It may not be realistic, but it certainly beats donning a pinny or unclogging drains.

The prescribed modern concept for the domestic goddess seems to promote aspirational creatures obsessing over their roll-top baths or creating show-off dinners that come garnished with peaks of saffron foam. Unfortunately, girls have not been encouraged to view domesticity as an excuse to indulge in wicked acts of slovenly behaviour as they relish the power of delegation. Domestic bliss is simple to achieve for a girl. You must furnish your abode liberally with passionate physical acts.

FRENCH MAID: DIRTY BUT CLEAN

A girl must be creative when it comes to tackling grime and dust. Banish thoughts that it's beneath you to get on your hands and knees to tend your floor, because this position can prove winning if you are in an amorous mood.

Cleaning in sexy underwear is very liberating and can brighten the day for you and the postman – you can be sure he will never expect a tip and will always knock twice.

I suggest a LBD with a white scalloped collar, ironic fluffy mules, a flimsy apron and fishnets, set off nicely with a kitsch duster for when you want your fancy tickled – such fun is lost on dust. This look can really help put a smile on a girl's face (and an even bigger grin on her lover's) when she has a spring clean, especially if she purrs into action with a soundtrack courtesy of 60s vixen Brigette Bardot.

Do remember if you are feeling overwhelmed by domesticity that Mr Muscle loves the jobs you hate, so why not see if you can pick up a helpful boy at the gym and set him to task on the cleaning, ironing and accounting. If Mr Muscle is not able to do a thorough enough job have Henry on stand-by stashed beneath your stairs, you will wonder at his ability to penetrate any hard-to-reach place and he is wonderfully adept at sucking.

If you are afraid a cleaner might steal from you, the solution is to hire nude male cleaners who can easily prove they have nothing to hide. Peace of mind is as important as provoking your neighbourhood curtain-twitchers.

Undertaking the Job in Hand

A girl should be prepared to use a little elbow grease when tackling certain jobs. Some are trickier and take longer than others, but if you really get stuck in, you will certainly reap a reward that gives you a glowing sense of pride.

A girl can add sparkle and vim to her bathroom with a good old-fashioned soapy wash, and when the word 'soapy' is mentioned by a girl a man's ears prick up from twenty feet away.

Wax on-wax off – must be done in the privacy of a girl's en suite or at her chosen salon, while the nice chap from the floor-cleaning company deals with shining up your wooden floors.

A girl should always strip her sheets regularly no matter how much of a slattern she is. Old tangled sex sheets are only worth keeping if you are a collector who likes edgy artists' conceptual work.

DIY 'DO IT... YOU!' — HOW TO GET OTHERS TO KEEP YOUR ABODE WELL MAINTAINED

When it comes to DIY ventures, unless power drills excite you I suggest you play dumb and solicit the energies of a chap who is good with his hands. After all, I bet you have grander designs to occupy yourself with and we all know men live to screw.

Motivating your worker needn't be difficult, just greet him at the door with a baked offering in the shape of a hammer and explain that when he is done you'd like to get nailed.

If your boy thinks of DIY as niche porn, give him an ironic boiler suit, 70s moustache and breathlessly tell him your pipes need looking at, before pointing him in the direction of the sink.

Useful Tips

Girls, it's valuable to remember that double-sided carpet tape works wonders for temporarily fastening objects to the spot or a suitor to the wall.

If your handyman accidentally prangs his wood during his endeavours do not fret, just use a wet cloth and a clothes iron to steam out the dent... don't forget to give him a stick to bite on.

If you are painting a wall, remember that the area will need to be primed first – if you are painting a man, use less toxic substances.

A girl can create the illusion of more space with plenty of mirrors, and she can create the illusion of being interested in DIY by showing rapturous appreciation for a boy's toolbox.

Tricky Issues

A girl should at the very least learn how to do one DIY job. For example, repairing a crack:

1. You must start by cleaning the affected area with a toothbrush and rubbing alcohol.

2. Apply sealing paste.

3. Sand until smooth before buffing.

4. Consult a doctor.

How can you create an indoor waterfall? If you are into that sort of thing then problem sorted, but make sure you have plenty of plastic sheeting and your cleaner is due the next day. For anything else talk to a builder.

Never involve yourself with fixing plumbing or electrical goods, because if there is a man in the vicinity it's better to take advantage of him. The only electricity a girl should engage with is based on pure chemistry.

If your suitor thinks you are not taking DIY tasks seriously, prove you can rise to the challenge by going on endless tea breaks, and tutting heavily at any shoddy workmanship, before taking off your shirt and shouting lewd suggestions at him. Congratulations, you are now an almost fully qualified builder.

DECOR(UM): SEDUCTIVE FURNISHINGS

It is important to make sure your home is a place you actively want to spend quality time in, whether alone or with company. Two simple things apply when creating a seductive, homely atmosphere – first that it looks tempting, and secondly that it smells delicious. These things help to stimulate intimacy.

Realistically most heterosexual boys' idea of seductive furnishings would comprise the largest home-entertainment system possible, a robot that serves beer and an armchair with a built-in remote. A seductive girl's home is thankfully a la-z-boy-free zone.

Tactile and attractive fabrics make your home a more alluring place to be, and what's sexier than a large velvet sofa that invites two naked lovers to christen it? A large leather couch is a close rival – it may not be as tantalising to your skin, but it still feels decadent and it's wipe clean.

Bedroom: The most seductive bedrooms are clutter-free, where the bed is king (or queen) size and opulently inviting. Stuffed toys are a no-no, but other toys are welcome as long as they are kept in a treasure chest at the foot of the bed. Too many pillows are not advised, as their removal rather kills any urgent acts of passion. A few unique, well-chosen pieces of art or artefacts that lend clues as to who you are and what your tastes are help to set off the overall effect.

Candles: Candlelight is a great deal more flattering and erotic than lights on a dimmer switch – the pretty flickering of the flame and the animalistic shadows it casts lend themselves beautifully to acts of intimacy. Expensive scented candles, which have wax which when liquid doubles as massage balm are particularly appealing.

Mirrors: Help to add further dimension to your room and to your seductions. You can be a player and a voyeur all at once.

Your bed: In feng shui it is said that the position of your bed can influence the type of sex life you have. For maximum mojo, line it against the wall opposite the door and it will lend potent sexual energy to your lair. Under no circumstances should your bed be in direct line with the door, as this is alarmingly known as 'the coffin' and that is certainly not the type of stiff you want in your boudoir.

Banish anything from your bedroom that could be classified as 'competition', for example things like laptops or televisions. At the very least, hide them when you have a suitor in tow. There is nothing worse than finding a chap secretly switching on *Match of The Day* when you are getting intimate; frankly the only box he should be engaged in is yours.

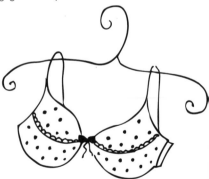

SUPER(MARKET) MODEL — GETTING CHECKED OUT AT THE CHECKOUT

"Supermarkets are more fascinating than any fashion salon."
WALLIS SIMPSON

A seductress can see the exotica of supermarkets, she knows they are not just establishments where old ladies and the harassed dash to get ready meals and gossip by the haddock. No, they are also thronging with sensual possibility.

Getting ready: Even if you are just popping out to your nearest convenience store, whether Harrods or Wal-Mart, a lady should look effortlessly gorgeous – you never know who you may bump into.

Mood music:
1. Pulp, 'Common People' ('I wanna sleep with common people like you, I said I'll see what I can do. I took her to a supermarket, I don't know why but I had to start it somewhere').

2. Bruce Springsteen's 'Queen of the Supermarket' ('I'm in love with the Queen of the Supermarket, As the evening sky turns blue, A dream awaits in aisle number 2').

3. Rick James 'Super Freak'... need I explain?

What to wear: Always create the you you want the world to see, be it bombshell, goddess, 1950s movie star, or effortless boho, though not if you are just popping out to the supermarket. You will get attention, but most men find women who are deliberately tarted-up when browsing bananas a bit of a turn-off. Sometimes less is more, so be casual in jeans and a tee by all means, but underneath luxuriate in the details with delicate Chantilly lace and sensual satin caressing your form.

Even in mufti you are a super(market) model and the aisles are your runways. If you couldn't leave the house without donning some hot vertiginous heels, use a shopping cart for extra balance and sashay forth.

Etiquette of the Supermarket

Harsh supermarket lighting should be a girl's enemy, but the seductress is aware that her own reflection in the aisles will be far from depressing and she will be a great lift to all who see her.

Show consideration when shopping by leaning into your trolley and showing a little more seamed thigh than the chap behind you had bargained for – this may cause him to spill his milk. No use crying over it.

For hard-to-reach items, ask a willing candidate to lend a helping hand – beware the security camera though.

A girl would never engage in trolley rage. Fighting over prime beef is so unseemly...

If the attendant offers to fill your bags and heave them to your car, don't forget the tip... How helpful have they been?

WHAT A MAN'S BASKET TELLS YOU ABOUT HIM:

Cheap ready meals for one, lads' magazines, tissues – there is a reason he lives alone!

Organic produce, vanilla, pineapple means he has impeccable taste... literally.

Gin, bourbon, codeine, ibuprofen, red lightbulbs and jam – certainly he is a curious creature.

Never on the Shelf

Supermarkets are seething with potential seduction. It is not a coincidence that in Australia single/dating nights are held in these venues. There is also the bonus of 24-hour supermarkets where all manner of night owls can be found picking up nocturnal goodies!

Aids to Seduction in Store

The cart/trolley: A perfect prop, lean into it, over it, dance around it, hide behind it, and for those with a more mischievous streak and fabulous pins, why not climb into the child seat and get a delicious Daddy to push you about?

Dirty dancing: Late at night or early in the day supermarket aisles with their seedily smooth piped tunes are perfect for practising your moves – use your trolley to bump your chosen partner and your body to grind.

Getting Fresh – Produce

Any girl who has ever seen Mickey Rourke and Kim Basinger ransack a fridge knows certain foods can bring out the gastro-erotic in people... apologise to the cleaner!

If you are not sure how to check whether a fruit is ripe, why not ask a knowledgeable-looking chap to help you, he will be only too happy to give your melons a good firm squeeze.

For a cheap or expensive thrill, indulge in a little sleight of hand. Shoplifting is the ultimate buzz for so many stars, so why not see what all the fuss is about? Start small and be casual and work your way up until risk becomes f-risk. Being manhandled into the foreboding back room by a cruel but just man will certainly get you thinking... he may not be a security guard!

UPSTAIRS DOWNSTAIRS — DEALING WITH STAFF

From *Lady Chatterley's Lover* to *Downton Abbey* there has always been a strong level of fantasy attached to the type of services domestic servants may provide.

Blurring the boundaries, though fun, can potentially be fraught with problems. Having your home-help luxuriating in your chamber rather than tidying it could eventually find you in the throes of a most unorthodox power struggle.

Your staff should be sourced only from the most reputable agencies or through someone you know, you wouldn't want just anyone tending to your intimates.

When Hiring a Domestic Aid

Make sure they have excellent credentials because lots of satisfied employers speaks volumes – also discretion and honesty give you the peace of mind that any airing of dirty laundry is your prerogative alone.

Let an employee know the rules and rewards of the job and present to them a contract entitled '50 Shades of Pay'.

A staff member who understands the importance of the personal touch is a precious thing. Quite how personal things become depends on you.

Au Pairs

If your paramour suggests a Swedish sex bomb as a nanny, it would be fair to question his motives – it's unlikely that he has your sprogs' cultural growth at the forefront of his mind. But if you do find an inappropriately sexy woman (other than yourself) looking after your progeny, ensure you bombard her with more seductive charm and respect than he can muster and she will be doggedly faithful to you.

Alternatively a girl should play her boy at his own game and interview a host of fit Brazilian mannies and see how he likes it.

Doggie-Man

It's sometimes not possible to give one's best friend all the exercise one should, especially if the office has been demanding. How wonderful that you can have an authoritative and loving chap come to your door and see that your little treasure gets to work off all its pent-up frustration. And if you are still begging for more, see if he will roll over and give you another bone. If you have a dog, make sure you take it for a good daily run around or pay someone else to.

Gardener

If you are not blessed with green fingers, then hiring a talented gardener to help your flora burst into life is money well spent. It's not surprising that hoes surround a man who spends his time planting his seed and lovingly tending to a girl's bush.

Being the boss doesn't mean that you shouldn't get to know your staff and build up good working relationships. A girl will find that anyone who helps around her household will prove a keeper if she offers praise for good work and reciprocates the respect and loyalty they afford her. But a girl should be consistent in how she treats her staff and what she asks them to do – if you have any special requests, broach the subject sensitively rather than taking advantage just because you pay a boy.

CHAPTER TEN

The final flirt:
five steps

The great thing about flirting is that you can do it anywhere with absolutely anyone who takes your fancy. It is the art behind making every element of a girl's life and interactions more joyful and exciting, and helps a girl to accrue freebies and invitations.

Flirting is one of the most widely employed and powerful social and seductive skills a boy or girl can use. A girl can flirt physically using her body to translate her intentions, or she can use written or verbal communication, and it may be that one of these forms works better for her than another.

When a girl flirts she is able to swiftly establish an air of intimacy with a relative stranger or use it as a tool to find out more about someone she is on more familiar terms with. Flirting does not have to lead to sex, but if that is your actual aim it is certainly a helpful place to start.

STEP ONE: THE PREY — SELECT YOUR MAN
If you purely want to hone your seductive techniques, then by all means flirt at will with any man you see fit. When it comes to serious seduction, you need to direct your attentions to a man you want to know more intimately. Who you choose is dictated by the chemical effect their aesthetics have on you.

You could meet that certain someone anywhere – in a lift, at a bar, at a social event or a gallery – so make sure you follow your instincts, and be cool and confident you won't let a good opportunity or man slip away.

STEP TWO: THE SIGNAL — GO
This is the part of seduction where more artful body language is used to increase the level of interplay. There are so many subtle signs being communicated by our bodies when we interact, so a girl needs to pay proper attention to the messages she is sending and the ones a boy is responding to, and act on these signals accordingly.

STEP THREE: THE HUNT — CHASE OR CHASTE?
In simple terms, when it comes to seduction a girl needs to know when she wishes to actively pursue a boy and when she would prefer to be pursued. Letting go of control can be extremely liberating, and equally men find it refreshing to

have a girl take charge, especially if she demonstrates through more obvious visual indicators what an irresistible creature she is.

STEP FOUR: THE PLAY – SHE GOT GAME
Toying with men too much is cruel, yet if you don't do it at all they start to wonder where all the fun and games went. There is a fine line between seductive flirting and wanting to step things up to actual sexual congress.

Using provocative or sexual dialogue in a light manner and allowing suggestiveness to gradually increase is a great way to test the boundaries of how far you can both go. The surest sign that proper intimacy is desirable is when both parties graduate from verbal dialogue to flirtatiously sensual touching.

STEP FIVE: THE KILL – THE FEMALE OF THE SPECIES IS MORE
DEADLY THAN THE MALE
When flirtatious touches have led to feverish kissing and you have negotiated your prey into the bedroom, you may find that just as you begin devouring a boy he may struggle, but remember he has willingly accepted his fate. Make sure you lead him to the edge of ecstasy before you finish him off. Don't feel bad for him, he certainly won't have suffered but will have felt every electrifying caress and kiss – quite frankly you should let him know it is your turn now...

Just as he is fading, a serene smile upon his face and events flashing before his eyes, pull him back from the brink. Nothing ensures a boy's glorious res-erection more swiftly than the good works of the seductress.

Good night girls and good luck!

First published in Great Britain in 2013 by
Pavilion Books, an imprint of
Anova Books
Old Magistrates Court
10 Southcombe Street
London W14 ORA

Cover image used with kind permission of *Harpers Bazaar*,
Hearst Magazines UK

Illustrations by Shutterstock

ISBN: 9781862059450

A CIP record for this book is available from
the British Library

Repro by Mission Productions Ltd, Hong Kong
Printed by 1010 Printing international Ltd, China.

Commissioning Editor: Emily Preece-Morrison
Copy Editor: Kate Turvey
Designer: Georgina Hewitt

10 9 8 7 6 5 4 3 2 1